Germany and Europe

The Crisis of Unity

David Marsh is the European Editor of the *Financial Times*. He is the author of two highly acclaimed, bestselling books on Germany, *The New Germany: At the Crossroads* and *The Bundesbank: The Bank that Rules Europe*.

DAVID MARSH

Germany and Europe

The Crisis of Unity

Mandarin

For Saskia and Sabrina

Photo credits
1, 2, 3, 5, 6, 8, 13, 14, 15 Bundesbildstelle, Bonn
9 Trevor Humphries Financial Times
11 Press Association
4, 10, 12 Reuter
7, 16, 17 Associated Press

A Mandarin Paperback
GERMANY AND EUROPE

First published in Great Britain 1994
by William Heinemann Ltd
This edition published 1995
by Mandarin Paperbacks
an imprint of Reed Consumer Books Ltd
Michelin House, 81 Fulham Road, London SW3 6RB
and Auckland, Melbourne and Singapore

Copyright © David Marsh 1994
The author has asserted his moral rights

A CIP catalogue record for this book is
available at the British Library
ISBN 0 7493 2007 9

Printed and bound in Great Britain
by Cox & Wyman, Reading, Berks.

Contents

Preface

The reassembly of Europe marked a positive beginning to the final decade of the twentieth century. Yet on the way illusions have been shattered along with states. Developments since 1989 include the disintegration of the Soviet Union and Yugoslavia, unleashing bloody regional wars; setbacks to the drive towards European political and economic union launched by the Maastricht treaty; the break-up of Czechoslovakia; the return to power of former communist parties in several central and east European countries; the collapse of Europe's system of fixed exchange rates; and a long western European recession, by some measures, the worst since the 1930s.

My aim in writing this book is to describe and explain the connections between the reforging of a united Germany and the diverse changes in the rest of the continent. This is in no sense a complete account of Europe's transition. Only in key places have I tried to give a detailed description of events as they unfolded. A central role in the narrative is inevitably played by Chancellor Helmut Kohl, elected for a fourth term in office – although with a drastically reduced majority – in October 1994.

I have shone a spotlight on German and European economic policy. The reunification of Germany, brought about, above all, by the East Germans' intense desire for better living standards, offers a fascinating example of the primacy of economics in the affairs of nations. Additionally, the European Community's attempts to handle the political aftermath of German unification laid stress on economic tools to bring about a new European equilibrium. The centrepiece of the Maastricht treaty was the plan for economic and monetary union, given backing particularly by France as a means of controlling Germany's economic power.

I have dealt only briefly with the changes in central and eastern Europe. However, the focus on Germany and the western part of the continent does not, I hope, obscure my view that Europe now has to be looked at as a whole. Europe's crucial task is to integrate central and eastern Europe as soon as possible into the European Community. When the EC agreed the Maastricht treaty, aimed at deepening the integration of western Europe rather than widening it to the East, it took a wrong turning.

Several factors will shift Europe in the direction of 'widening' in coming years. United Germany's economic problems have diminished – though not eliminated – its neighbours' fears of a dominant Germany that has to be 'anchored' at all costs in the European Community. The setbacks encountered by the Maastricht project will inevitably delay 'deepening'. The enlargement of the EC in January 1995 to include Sweden, Finland and Austria adds to the momentum behind proposals to open membership to the Czech republic, Hungary and Poland.

These prospective eastern members all have relatively low incomes and large agricultural sectors. So allowing them to join the EC – even with lengthy transition periods to limit their immediate access to EC funds – will be prohibitively expensive unless the EC makes further efforts to reform its budgetary procedures, particularly the Common Agricultural Policy. Since the economic aftermath of unification has exacerbated German budgetary problems, Germany will be in the vanguard of efforts to lower the EC's financial ambitions during the next decade.

The continent's economy will recover only slowly from the recession that lamed initiative and dampened spirits between 1991 and 1993. Unless the European Community shows more sure-footedness than in the years immediately after the end of the Cold War, the risk of weakness will grow. Europe's strength has always been its diversity of talents, energies and cultures. This diversity is now being put to the test; it must be made to work.

I have benefited from much help and many conversations throughout Europe in writing this book. A record of interviews is found in the Notes section. I thank many colleagues at the *Financial Times* for stimulating insights that have greatly aided my analysis. I am very grateful to Anthony Evans, Arthur Goodhart, Thomas Mayer, Michael Mertes and Holger Schmieding for their assistance and comments on the manuscript and thank, too, Tom Weldon and Emma Rhind-Tutt of Heinemann. As always I owe a huge debt to my wife Veronika.

David Marsh, Wimbledon, November 1994

Note on Terms

- The twelve member states which have adhered to the Treaty of Rome call themselves the 'European Union' following the ratification of the Maastricht treaty in November 1993. However, this book refers to them as the 'European Community' (abbreviated to EC). There are three reasons for this. First, much of the text refers to the European Community as it existed in the past, when to call it anything else would plainly be wrong. Second, the legal term for the 'twelve' remains European Community, not European Union. Third, the 'Community' is plainly not yet a 'union', and to pretend otherwise is unnecessary and misleading.

- 'West Germany' refers both to the Federal Republic of Germany as it existed before 3 October 1990, and to the western part of today's united Germany. Similarly, 'East Germany' refers both to the pre-1990 state of the German Democratic Republic and to the eastern part of the reunited nation.

- 'Reunification' and 'unification' are used interchangeably to refer to the act of bringing together East and West Germany. Although some German politicans and commentators have insisted that 'reunification' should be used only to denote the reforging of the pre-1945 Reich, this has always seemed an example of unhelpful sophistry.

- One billion means one thousand million. One trillion means one thousand billion.

- Exchange rates: £1 = DM2.50.

Dramatis personae

Adenauer, Konrad. West German chancellor, 1949–63.

Baker, James. US secretary of state 1989–92.

Balladur, Edouard. French finance minister, 1986–88. Prime minister, 1993–.

Bérégovoy, Pierre. French finance minister, 1984–86, 1988–92. Prime minister, 1992–93.

Brandt, Willy. West German foreign minister, 1966–69. Chancellor, 1969–74.

Bush, George. US president, 1989–93.

Delors, Jacques. French finance minister, 1982–84. President of European Commission, 1985–94.

Erhard, Ludwig. West German economics minister, 1949–63. Chancellor, 1963–66.

de Gaulle, Charles. French president, 1958–69.

Genscher, Hans-Dietrich. West German foreign minister, 1974–90. German foreign minister, 1990–92.

Giscard d'Estaing, Valéry. French president, 1973–81.

Gorbachev, Mikhail. Soviet Communist Party general secretary, 1985–91. President, 1988–91.

Honecker, Erich. East German Communist Party general secretary, 1971–89.

Krenz, Egon. East German Communist Party general secretary, 1989.

Kohl, Helmut. West German chancellor 1982–90. German chancellor, 1990–.

de Maizière, Lothar. East German prime minister, 1990.

Major, John. British prime minister, 1990–.

Modrow, Hans. East German prime minister, 1989–90.

Mitterrand, François. French president, 1981–.

Pöhl, Karl Otto. Bundesbank president 1980–91.

Schlesinger, Helmut. Bundesbank president 1991–93.

Schmidt, Helmut. West German chancellor, 1974–82.
Tietmeyer, Hans. Bundesbank president 1993–.
Thatcher, Margaret. British prime minister, 1979–90.
Waigel, Theo. West German finance minister, 1989–90. German finance minister, 1990–.

Glossary

Bonn Convention (*Deutschlandvertrag*). Treaty establishing West Germany as sovereign state. Took effect in 1955.

Bundesbank. German central bank, statutorily independent, established in 1957, replacing Bank deutscher Länder.

Council of Ministers. Main EC decision-making body, made up of ministers from each EC member government.

Deutsche Mark (DM). West Germany currency, created in June 1948. Became currency of East and West Germany in July 1990.

East Mark (EM). Inconvertible East German currency. Dissolved in July 1990.

European central bank. Central bank planned to run single European currency.

Economic and monetary union (Emu). Planned system of irrevocably fixed European exchange rates leading to a single currency. First proposed in 1962, with goal reiterated in 1970. Under Maastricht treaty, to be established at the latest in 1999.

European Commission. Brussels-based civil service, led by twenty commissioners (including a president), which initiates and administers EC legislation.

European Community (EC). Grouping of fifteen European states that have established a system of economic and political cooperation which, under Maastricht treaty, could become a form of confederation. Members: original signatories of Treaty of Rome plus UK, Ireland, Denmark (joined 1973), Greece (1981), Spain, Portugal (1986), Austria, Finland and Sweden joined in 1995.

European Monetary Institute (EMI). Forerunner of planned European central bank, formed to improve cooperation among existing central banks. Started during autumn 1994 in Frankfurt.

European Monetary System (EMS). Exchange rate stabilisation scheme, started in March 1979, under which fluctuation bands were set for most European Community currencies.

European parliament. A 567-member, directly elected body with the right to veto or amend EC legislation, control budget and supervise European Commission.

European Union (EU). Name for EC in Maastricht treaty.

Exchange rate mechanism (ERM). EMS fluctuation bands for EC currencies, widened to 15 per cent in August 1993.

German (re)unification. Took effect on 3 October 1990.

Maastricht treaty. Amendment to Treaty of Rome setting route to political union, agreed by EC leaders in December 1991, came into effect in November 1993.

North Atlantic Treaty Organisation (Nato). A defence grouping of sixteen nations, linking US, Canada and West European states. Set up in 1949 on basis of Treaty of Brussels (1948).

Relations treaty. Treaty that took effect between East and West Germany in 1972, allowing recognition as separate states.

Single European Act. Amendment to Treaty of Rome establishing principle of single market, allowing EC to take decisions in Council of Ministers by majority voting. Took effect in 1987.

Single Market. Barrier-free market allowing free movement of goods, people, capital and services, across EC from January 1993.

Treaty of Rome. Treaty signed in 1957 establishing European Economic Community (later EC) among Belgium, Italy, France, Luxembourg, Netherlands and West Germany.

1

Europe's Heartbeat

In helping Germany achieve freedom and unity, I believe all the states and peoples of Europe can be the winners. That should be our aim.

James Baker, US Secretary of State, 1990 [1]

As a man from the East I really believed that when we had got rid of communism, all our problems would be over. In the Rhineland, they tell the joke: 'Why do the Chinese smile? Because they still have the Wall.' It is dreadful, dreadful. We should be saying: 'Why are we Germans smiling? Because we no longer have the Wall.'

Joachim Meisner, Archbishop of Cologne, 1993 [2]

We Germans are in the midst of one of the greatest tests in our history. Our partners in the European Community, our neighbours in Europe, the whole world expects from us that we muster the necessary solidarity among our own people to meet the challenge.

Helmut Schmidt, former West German Chancellor, 1993 [3]

I

When Berlin's Cold Wall crumbled, the Cold War edifice of Europe collapsed, sending aloft a dust cloud of uncertainty that has refused to settle. In 1989–90, Europe triumphed over the forces that disrupted and despoiled the continent and the German nation at its heart. In the fifth decade after the ending of the Second World War, the heart started to beat again.

For the victors, communism's death brought a sting. Europe and Germany again became whole and free. Yet since the breaching of the concrete barrier across Berlin they have grown unquiet. German unification, according to the aspirations of many governments, was to have accelerated the process of European political and economic union. In fact, although Europe in East and West stands joined by a new interdependence, the effect of German unity has proved an obstacle rather than a catalyst for the unification of the continent. The main elements of European power will remain Europe's nation-states. In their midst lies a reborn Germany, larger now, but made uneasy by the trials of adjustment to internal strains and to its new place in the world.

The disintegration of the superpower blocs and the

3

break-up of the Soviet Union have lifted the partition of the continent, but generated new fragmentation. After their victory over communism, Nato and the European Community face a fresh test. In losing their adversary, they also relinquished a source of strength. The fear that for forty years kept the West in thrall, of nuclear conflict unleashed by totalitarian might, has faded. In its place has grown a patchwork of smaller antagonisms and threats. Regions such as the former Yugoslavia, freed from the pull of larger forces, have returned to the grip of ancient rivalries. The fall of the Soviet empire has extinguished the ideological and military struggle that seared the post–1945 world. Yet the snuffing out of superpower confrontation has enfeebled those who previously stood closest to the flame. The preponderance of western liberal capitalism is unchallenged, but the alliance of ideals and self-interest among its exponents has become weaker and less sure.

Europe's post-Cold War road has run a zigzag course across a terrain made unfamiliar through having been submerged for four decades by the now-ebbed tide of - Soviet imperialism. Few foresaw that the balance between risk and reward would prove so precarious, and that so many would lose their footing along the way. Nowhere has the route been as entangled as in Germany, the pivot of Europe, and also its reflection. If Europe prospers, so too will Germany; without a healthy Germany, there can be no healthy Europe. United Germany emerged larger in population and in territory than the old Federal Republic, but weaker in political balance, in economic structure, in ability to govern itself, in capacity to exert patient influence on its neighbours. The Federal Republic's economy increased by 7 per cent; its inhabitants, 25 per cent; its geographical area,

40 per cent; its unemployment rate, 50 per cent; its problems, 100 per cent. Germany and Europe will be dogged, to the end of the century and beyond, by the perils and pains of transition.

With unification, the coffin lid closed on the German Democratic Republic: ill-loved, ill-formed, ill-named. Few Germans in the West mourned its passing. But they would miss its enduring presence, for its image had been a comforting reminder of West Germany's prowess, stability and good fortune. These were attributes that made unification feasible. Ironically, once it took effect, they were destined to be diminished. East Germany's existence under Soviet sponsorship and misrule had exacted retribution for Germany's responsibility for the Second World War, and for its ultimate defeat. In 1989–90, East Germany met its demise, yet the sense of retribution lingered. Stalinism sent a shadow beyond the grave that impedes and darkens the footsteps of the renascent nation.

For the Germans in the East, the extinction of their state stirred a still more complex ferment of emotions. East Germany bequeathed debts – psychological, political, economic – that had to be repaid. It left scars, formed during its four decades of existence, that were likely to take as long again to heal. Unification was fervently desired by the broad mass of the East German people, and when it came, they rejoiced. Yet they set out on an unsettling voyage.

The seedy, paternalistic despotism of the East German regime had been an oppressive, often brutal force, but it had nurtured solidarity and fellow-feeling among those it had encumbered. When the system was stripped away, the people discovered that the police state's elaborate network of information, surveillance and control had seeped into virtually every home. Just as the wave of D-Marks surging through the Berlin Wall increased living standards but destroyed jobs, the opening up of files showing the extent of East Germans' collaboration with the state security apparatus brought both illumination and shame. Solidarity evaporated as rapidly as the hope that adjustment to the rigours of market economics would be painless. As reality crowded in, the Germans in the East had to come to terms not only with the sudden changes in their present circumstances, but also with uncomfortable reminders of a past many had hoped quickly to forget.

Released from the hold of the Soviet Union into the more benign custody of the West, 16 million East Germans were freed from oppression. But they were subjected to a new form of dependence: this time towards their 63 million rich neighbours who, with growing reluctance, started to channel eastwards an annual DM150 billion in fiscal resources and subsidies, largely to support consumption in what became known as the new *Länder* (federal states).[4]

There was a peculiar symmetry at work, since these financial flows caused equal discontent on both sides. Financed by increased taxes, as well as heavy borrowing on the bond markets, the cash pumped eastwards caused sizeable cuts in West German incomes. Yet, since it was impossible to use fiscal redistribution to bring East German living standards fully up to West German levels, the transfers were not large enough to counter strong disillusionment in the East over the aftermath of unification. One factor, above all, increased the East Germans' resentment: the westerners' expectation that the recipients of this largesse should show gratitude. It was hardly surprising that, according to an opinion poll in 1993, only one-fifth of Germans in the West, and one-tenth of those in the East, registered a spirit of national 'togetherness' across the Elbe.[5]

II

These large internal transfers represented just one way in which unification transformed the face of Germany. Within and beyond its borders, the nation was exposed to a profusion of frequently contradictory expectations and objectives. Facing up to these challenges one by one would be an arduous task; to fulfil them all was not possible. The proliferation of demands resulted partly from anticipation abroad that a united Germany would automatically enlarge its economic and political dominance in Europe. In the light of Germany's bellicose history during the previous 130 years, some of these views were understandable. In fact, foreign perceptions of an extension of German might, and the confidence of many West German politicians that reunification would be relatively free of stress, proved mutually reinforcing. Strengthened not by calm judgement but by unthinking repetition, the Bonn government's well-broadcast belief that the obstacles of unification could be overcome within a few years contributed to a sizeable overstretching of German resources.

The Bonn government reacted to the confusion of expectations not by drawing up a clear list of priorities, but by suggesting that Germany could somehow meet them all. Hans-Dietrich Genscher, foreign minister at the time of unification, who was born in Halle in East Germany and held the foreign affairs portfolio in Bonn for eighteen years, personified Germany's all-consuming desire to keep its policy contours blurred in a haze of universal goodwill. Genscher, who retired in 1992, was the pivotal figure in the liberal Free Democratic Party, the Bonn coalition partner of Chancellor Helmut Kohl's conservative Christian Democratic Union. In 1990, Kohl, the burly politician of unshakeable certainties from the Rhineland-Palatinate region of south-west Germany, and Genscher, the Svengali-like figure[6] from the East, formed the vital partnership driving Germany to unification. The new Germany, according to both Genscher and Kohl, would exert not 'power' but 'responsibility'[7] through what Genscher called 'a policy of the good example'. It soon became clear that the quality of each example would be measured in hard cash. Foreign disquiet about Germany's new-found strength would be dissipated by plentiful supplies of D-Marks.

The German government committed itself to increasing economic assistance to the poorer parts of the European Community as part of the move towards European political and economic union. The centrepiece was a plan to reduce the monetary dominance of the Bundesbank, the German central bank, and ultimately to replace the D-Mark by a single European currency. This was an important concession; but the German government was bidding for a still more important prize. To smooth the passage of German unity, Bonn wanted to show its neighbours that the new Germany would be as firmly bound as the old Federal Republic to the concept of European integration. French and British agreement to German unification was crucial. Together with the other former Second World War allies, the United States and Soviet Union, France and the UK in 1990 had formal responsibility for settling the outcome of the 'German Question' left unresolved at the end of the war. By agreeing to monetary union, in the treaty eventually agreed at Maastricht in the Netherlands in December 1991, Germany helped win assent to unification.

However, when agreeing to give up the D-Mark in favour of a single European currency, the Bonn government knew it would not have to deliver on this promise until towards the end of the 1990s. As it has turned out, the road from Maastricht has run into an increasing number of stumbling blocks; these make it likely that the destination of full-scale European monetary union, if reached at all, will not be attained until the twenty-first century.

The changes in German circumstances raised expectations from other quarters too. The newly liberated states of eastern Europe hoped that a united Germany would provide finance and expertise to speed their transformation into market-orientated economies. The aspiration was understandable. Had not West Germany undergone a similar metamorphosis, under what seemed in retrospect to have been similarly difficult conditions, in the years immediately after the Second World War? The Soviet leadership, for its part, successfully pressed requests for DM15 billion in aid as one of the conditions for repatriating its troops from East Germany. The demand seemed acceptable. By 1994 the Red Army was to withdraw 380,000 soldiers from a land it had held for half a century – a territory that had represented the prize for the decisive Soviet contribution to defeating Hitler. Surely a few billion D-Marks was a worthwhile price for the release of a territory whose recovery, a decade earlier, would have been accomplished only at the cost of a third world war?

Calculated individually, the size of the required financial outlays did not appear excessive, when set against the potential resources of a united Germany and against the perception that unification would lead to sustained economic growth. Yet by 1994, after the immediate post-unity economic stimulus had given way to a sharp recession, the country that was the focus of these diverse demands seemed incapable of meeting them.

During the 1990s, the West Germans will be transferring every year to the eastern part of the nation cash resources equivalent to 5 per cent of West Germany's total income: an unprecedented obligation for any modern nation in peacetime. As one Hungarian economist laconically commented in 1994: 'The West no longer has any reason to fear German dominance. The East Germans have resolved the problem.'[8] The size of the burden partly represented the legacy of communism. It also reflected, however, a succession of errors since 1990 in handling the economics and politics of unification. Some of these mistakes were inevitable; others could have been avoided. On the eve of Unity Day on 3 October 1990, even Kohl was plagued by residual doubts about the journey ahead, warning of the risk that Germany could be split into 'givers' in the West and 'takers' in the East.[9] Kohl was unable to translate diagnosis into decisions. The chancellor's road to unity was also his path to hubris.

III

Nine months before its fortieth anniversary in 1989, Erich Honecker, East Germany's seventy-six-year-old long-time leader, forecast that the Berlin Wall would survive another fifty or hundred years.[10] This was miscalculation of a grandiose kind. Many in the West, too, held the view that East Germany – for all its unsavouriness – had earned its place on the map of Europe: a position that seemed assured both by the superpowers' reluctance to see it disappear, and by its proficiency as the best-performing economy in the Soviet bloc.

Official East Berlin figures on industrial output may have been implausible, but West Germany generally preferred to believe them. If there were grounds for scepticism about East German statistics, culled, for instance, from intelligence reports or from information from the one-fifth of East Germany's population who had emigrated to the West since its foundation in 1949, then West Germany had no great desire to make them public. The Germans in East and West were, after all, interested in stable relations; indulging in self-aggrandisement at East Germany's expense would have set back this objective. Furthermore, West German ministers, industrialists, bankers and trade unionists were genuinely impressed by their earnest discussions, ostensibly as equals, at biannual Leipzig industrial fairs; by the East Germans' efforts in investing billions of East Marks in four-megabit memory chips; and, last but not least, by their athletes' extraordinary medal-winning sporting achievements. If anyone could make communism work, then – it seemed reasonable to believe – it would be the Germans. This confidence in the East's effectiveness persisted for several months after unification. The West Germans misjudged the resilience of the country that crumbled into their arms.

Another significant mistake concerned not East but West Germany. It concerned the structure and competitiveness of the German economy. Just as the East's basic economic strength had been overestimated, so too was that of the West. In the immediate aftermath of unity, this fundamental German weakness was masked from view. When reality finally hit home, in 1993-94, large-scale layoffs throughout German industry represented the only way to repair the damage.

Already in the late 1980s, critical voices had been raised in West Germany over the need to overhaul an economic system that, for all its post-war success, was starting to grow inflexible, costly and uncompetitive. West Germany's consensus-based system of economic and political management had greatly contributed to stability and prosperity. Yet there were signs that it was failing to cope, on the domestic front, with the rising demands of the welfare state and, internationally, with the economic challenges posed by cost-cutting and deregulation in the US, Asia and the rest of Europe.

The proponents of this thesis feared that Germany, for all its appearance of wealth and competence, was facing a period of gradual decline.[11] Martin Bangemann, economics minister in 1988, summed up the anxiety by quoting lines from Thomas Mann's novel *Buddenbrooks*:

> The outward, visible and tangible signs and symbols of happiness and achievement often appear only when in reality everything is already starting to go downhill again. The outer signs take time to arrive – like the light of a star that shines most brightly when it is on the way to being extinguished, or maybe has already gone out.[12]

However, any firm intention on the part of government or industry to tackle this issue faded quickly into the background as, from 1989-90 onwards, Germany embarked on the adventure of unification. As West German industry rapidly built up investments in East

German distribution outlets and production facilities, and the government greatly expanded the budget deficit in what was complacently termed 'start-up financing',[13] the German economy was buoyed by a classic Keynesian demand stimulus. Worries about fading competitiveness melted in the heat of the unity boom. The consequences of unity did not, however, remove the need for reform of the West German economy; they merely postponed it.

Worse, West Germany's failure to take heed of the warnings voiced at the end of the 1980s added greatly to East Germany's economic and social difficulties. Rather than restructuring a system for running the economy that was already showing signs of grave shortcomings, West Germany exported it across the Elbe – to an area ill-equipped to cope with it.

The introduction of the D-Mark in 1990 at an exchange rate that represented an enormous overvaluation of the East German Mark, together with instant membership of the European Community, exposed East Germany's moribund industrial enterprises to the full force of western competition. The best companies in the US, Japan and Europe were thirsting for market share in a territory that had previously been closed to capitalism. It quickly became evident that perhaps three-quarters of East Germany's outmoded factories would have to be shut down and replaced by up-to-date industrial investment. What was not clear, however, was how much the advent of West Germany's tightly regulated, high-cost economic system would by itself impede the necessary process of adjustment.

East Germany's competitiveness problems were exacerbated by unrealistically high East German wage increases in the three years after unity, as well as by the rapid collapse of trade within the former communist countries. East Germany's exports to the Comecon trading area of the Soviet bloc declined sharply as long-term trade agreements were unravelled. Additionally, the opening of eastern and central Europe to capitalism brought, for the first time, a Hong Kong-style manufacturing challenge to Germany's doorstep. The whole of German industry was subject to low-cost industrial competition from this rapidly liberalising region. While this had a beneficial impact in promoting necessary adjustment among parts of West German industry, it had severe consequences in East Germany. Many western companies, taking advantage of much lower labour costs in other erstwhile communist countries, leap-frogged East Germany and implemented their investment plans instead in Hungary, Poland or the Czech republic.

This juxtaposition of unfortunate, though not totally unforeseeable, circumstances greatly handicapped prospects for recovery east of the Elbe, setting off a spiral of negative repercussions. East Germany's economic plight increased demand for fiscal transfers. These financial flows swelled government spending and budget deficits. The budgetary imbalance triggered higher Bundesbank interest rates. These, in turn, contributed to the severity of Germany's 1993 recession, further complicating the task of bringing the newly liberated East towards economic and political normality.

Pre-unification West Germany had been one of the most wealthy and homogeneous states in the European Community. East Germany, by contrast, immediately became the Community's largest depressed region, poorer in economic output than southern Italy and most parts of Greece.[14] As a result, united Germany became one of the most economically and socially polarised states in Europe. In 1991, economic output per head in the five new East German *Länder*, comprising 18 per cent of the population, was 35 per cent or less of the European Community average. By 1995, the East German economy was growing at the fastest rate in the European Community, and yet output per head was still less than half that in West Germany.

The German government attempted to bridge the divide by promising in 1990 that East Germans would soon accede to West German living standards. The target was politically opportune, but economically foolhardy, for it was unlikely to be achieved in less than a generation. As in the field of foreign policy, the gap between the hopes invested in united Germany and the nation's ability to fulfil them was alarmingly wide. It was a combination that could only increase the potential for discord in the years ahead.

IV

Germany stands at the confluence of European ideas and European energy. Changing currents in Germany send out ripples that wash back again as a tranquil stream or a roaring flood. Nowhere are questions about the shape and direction of Europe raised with greater insistence than in the nation at its centre. In no other country does the pattern of political and economic events have a greater impact on its neighbours' destiny. Although the whole of the European economy benefited from the initial acceleration of economic growth in the wake of unity, Germany's subsequent difficulties resounded throughout the continent.

The unification of Germany and the collapse of the

Soviet Union were cathartic events for which the West was profoundly grateful, and profoundly unprepared. Western governments failed to realise that the crisis of decay and decline in the communist empire would, in western Europe, create an almost equally severe crisis of adjustment. They did not realise that the pain accompanying the consequent overhaul of West European structures would diminish ordinary people's enthusiasm for political and economic union. They did not anticipate that the Maastricht plan to replace the D-Mark by a single European currency would hinder rather than spur Europe's reconstruction.

Germany is the only member of the European Community to have been physically transformed. But across western Europe, the upheavals in the East have changed the mood of nations. The climate of questioning of incumbent governments and institutions across the continent was profoundly linked to the demise of communism.

Would the withering of British self-confidence in the early 1990s have been so severe had not the 1991-92 recession coincided with the end of Britain's Cold War position as guardian and guarantor of a divided continent? The UK may have felt less comfortable than its EC partners in gearing its future to that of the rest of Europe. None the less, the reduction in relative importance of Britain's political and economic ties to the rest of the world (including the US) left Britain with little choice. There is no doubt that Margaret Thatcher's attempts, as strident as they were futile, to hold up German unification contributed to the decline of her reputation in the final twelve months of her premiership and her resignation in November 1990. Britain's post-war European role collapsed at the same time as a leader who had been uniquely inspired by Britain's wartime glories.

Germany's reunification difficulties greatly complicated the life of Margaret Thatcher's successor. Tying sterling to the D-Mark in Europe's exchange rate stabilisation scheme, the European Monetary System, was a pivotal part of John Major's economic policies. Yet the link was shattered when the pound was forced out of the system in September 1992 under the impact of high Bundesbank interest rates. Major's government could not escape opposing fears of being ensnared in a German-dominated 'federal' Europe, and of being excluded from a 'core' of richer countries, led by France and Germany, forging ahead with integration on their own.

France was the perennial focus of British worries about a privileged partnership with Germany. However, German unification brought the Paris government a decisively changed environment for policy-making. Under the post-war Fourth and Fifth Republics, France had striven to maintain equilibrium in the European Community between French and German economic prowess and political interests. German unity, by unsettling the balance of Europe, destroyed the balance of French policies.

As the two disparate German states came together again, President François Mitterrand, like Thatcher, sensed a return to instability. Like that of the British prime minister, Mitterrand's standing, too, was diminished by his attempts in 1989-90 to forestall unification. It suffered still more from his embarrassing underestimation, at the time of the Soviet coup in August 1991, of reformist pressures in the Soviet Union. Mitterrand became a principal advocate of coupling the French franc to the D-Mark, in an effort to counter German dominance by building economic and monetary union. However, in trying to break the mould of the European monetary order, France ended up being trapped in it. After the EMS upsets of autumn 1992 and, particularly, the summer 1993 unrest when the franc came under unprecedented pressure, it was evident that France's strategy had only served to confirm the Bundesbank's domination of European money.

The shifts in Europe's economic and political landscape had repercussions too on the southern nations. In Italy, the upheavals helped precipitate the splintering of the old state and party structures that had maintained the country for so long in their grip. As long as the Soviet empire held sway, a tacit alliance of forces (including the Mafia and the US State Department) provided Italy's Christian Democrats with a permanent stake in power, sustained by a wide-spun network of financial malpractice and illicit power-bargaining. The depth of political corruption revealed in 1992-93 discredited the former political establishment of both Left and Right, resulting in their comprehensive ejection and the advent of new and untried parties in the March 1994 elections, led by the Forza Italia party of media magnate Silvio Berlusconi. The collapse of the Italian system – almost as thoroughgoing as the disintegration of regimes in eastern Europe – came about because of the impatience of the Italian electorate with its waste and perniciousness. Impatience alone, however, would have been insufficent to dislodge it, had the metamorphosis of Europe not made it redundant.

Among the newer members of the Community, Spain and Portugal saw their fortunes wane in the early 1990s, partly in view of increased competition from the East in the fight to attract foreign investors and European Community funding. An extension of Community membership to central and eastern Europe by the end of the century would transfer EC resources to the East away from the continent's Mediterranean belt. The countries of the Iberian peninsula have no choice but to try to reform economic structures with redoubled energy. Otherwise, as the continent's centre of gravity shifts, they will again suffer from their location on Europe's south-west periphery.

V

As change reverberated around Europe, united Germany was unable to pursue a new set of policies to meet the dramatic alterations in its circumstances. Could any other outcome, however, have been expected? During forty post-war years, the Federal Republic, closely integrated with the West, had grown wealthy, comfortable, and indecisive. Modern Germany had renounced the art and practice of strategic planning: its specialisation was no longer motorised war but motorised holidays. Colonialisation was accomplished not with blood and iron but through the export of washing machines and high-powered cars. When German citizens sought *Lebensraum*, their aspiration was not conquest of foreign lands but a place for their elderly relatives in old people's homes. After Hitler's excesses, this was a country of efficiency and self-effacement that had won approval and respect abroad. It was not one, however, likely to carry out the radical reordering of national priorities made necessary by the epic challenge of unification.

The hallmark of united Germany is hesitancy, not heroism. The politicians who presided over unification were diminished by its consequences; no statesmen came to the fore to take their place. Prevarication, not potency, is on display. In one of the few foreign policy areas where united Germany has made a clear-cut decision – in pressing the Community to give diplomatic recognition to Croatia in December 1991 – the outcome was a pitiful failure. Germany has regained national sovereignty but is unsure what to do with it. It can produce a well-ordered diagnosis of the ailments of the East German economy, but it cannot enact a cure. It pronounces good intentions to take a higher profile on the world stage, for instance in allowing Bundeswehr troops to take part in international peace-keeping missions, but it cannot turn such ideas into results. It has more room now to deploy national interests, but cannot define what they are.[15]

For several years to come, opportunities for cohesive government in Germany will be constrained, while room for irresolution will grow. By overcoming division, Germany threw off the longest-lasting legacy of the Second World War. But its hopes of rapidly becoming a 'normal' European nation are unlikely to be fulfilled. It is beset less by the burdens of the past than by the burdens of the present. Germany built post-war recovery on exports, yet many important industrial sectors have run into great competitiveness difficulties. It has more neighbours than any other European country, yet it runs the risks of turning its gaze inward. For those who feared a flexing of German muscles, does this pattern of events provide a source of comfort . . . or a warning? If Germany ever again becomes a threat to European stability, the danger is likely to stem not from German strength, but from German weakness.

2

The Melting of
the Ice

Fifty million free citizens of the Federal Republic are at this hour thinking with brotherly love of millions of other Germans who are still forced to dwell, separated from us, in thralldom and in lawlessness. We hail them: you belong to us, we belong to you.

Konrad Adenauer, West German Chancellor, 1955[1]

Our adversaries find socialism on German soil so intolerable because the previously exploited masses have proved they can determine their fate without capitalists.

Erich Honecker, General Secretary,
East German Socialist Unity Party (SED), 1989[2]

East Germany's tragedy is that we have had no time to come to terms with and reflect on our forty-year history. We won our sovereignty on 9 November, and we are giving it up again on 2 July.*

Walter Romberg, East German Finance Minister, 1990

* Planned date for entry into force of German monetary union.

I

The story of Germany's separation and reunification is a contorted tale: an arduous passage down fateful paths and unexpected turnings. Through the chain of events connecting capitulation on 8 May 1945 to the fusion of East and West Germany on 3 October 1990 runs a thread of contradictory policies and emotions. Germany's post-1945 partition resulted not from a post-war peace treaty, but from the failure to enact one; not from a firm strategy by the victors of the Second World War, but from its absence. West Germany's 1949 constitution proclaimed 'the unity and freedom of Germany' as the supreme national goal.[4] Yet many came progressively to fear that an attempt to realise it might overturn all that the country had built up in forty years. The ending of division illustrated the strangest paradox of all. The nation could become whole again only once it had ceased to think and behave as a nation.

Despite the Allies' wartime plan to set up zones of occupation in defeated Germany, dismemberment was not part of their original intentions. Above all to ease payment of reparations, the US, Britain and the Soviet Union pledged at the Potsdam conference in August 1945 to treat occupied Germany 'as a single economic unit'. However, as the anti-Hitler coalition split in acrimony and then enmity in the years afterwards, the western and eastern parts of Germany were suspended, and then sealed, in the force-field of US–Soviet confrontation. The end of Hitler's war, and the apparent stability of the political constellation in Europe that followed it, seemed, for a time, to bring the end of German history. With a sense of both resignation and relief, a renowned American dictionary in 1987 defined Germany as 'a former country in central Europe'.[5] The corollary was that East Germany was described in a book published in the UK in 1988 as 'perhaps the most stable socialist state in Eastern Europe.'[6]

The two German states established in 1949 were Cold War children, each subject to the pull of its respective superpower. When the ice melted, few realised how strong would be the forces drawing them together again. Upon unification, one reached adulthood, the other expired. The zeal with which many West Germans had previously convinced themselves and the world that reunification was impossible was swiftly channelled into making the chimera reality.[7] Fulfilment of the dream brought both rejoicing and a rude awakening. The gravitational attraction between the two Germanys was between unequal objects, and was generated by unequal motivations. In the reforged halves of Germany, it was to have highly unequal effects.

As long as the bipolar superpower system remained in place, the German Democratic Republic did not look unstable. Once radical signs of *détente* between the US and the Soviet Union became evident in 1988-89, East Germany's weakness became increasingly exposed. However, in a parallel miscalculation in East and West, neither of the two German states seemed aware of the full extent of mounting economic and political pressure in East Berlin. Having supplied a large part of the hard currency assistance on which East Germany's relative economic prowess within the Soviet bloc was based, Bonn took a certain pride in East Germany's official statistics showing it had become one of the world's top ten industrial nations. The shock was all the greater when the world discovered the shallowness of East Germany's foundations. As Chancellor Kohl put it in 1990, 'For a long period, East Germany appeared a monolith. But it was a house of cards, and it simply fell down.'[8]

The Germans' lack of preparation for reunification hampered the chances of mastering the consequences. Yet unpreparedness played a vital role in making it possible. Without tacit acceptance in the 1970s and 1980s by successive Bonn governments, led by both Social Democrats and Christian Democrats, that German division was part of the post-war European *status quo*, relations between the US and Soviet Union would never have improved sufficiently to allow the *status quo* to be overturned.

Before the breaching of the Berlin Wall on 9 November 1989, neither Kohl nor anyone else possessed anything remotely resembling an operational plan for German unification. Had an overt strategy existed to change a state of affairs accepted as a principal outcome of the Second World War, it would have crumbled under an onslaught of suspicion and opposition at home and abroad. Kohl himself possessed no special foresight to prepare himself for an event that, for so many Germans, had been the object of indeterminate desire, yet which so few believed they would witness.[9]

Throughout his political career, Kohl continually affirmed his belief in 'national unity'. With a doggedness unmatched by any other leading German politician, he regularly restated his belief that the lives and destinies of the people east of the Elbe were a matter of shared German responsibility. However, for all his well-practised statements that time would somehow bring the Germans back together, *Wiedervereinigung* (reunification) for many years was not part of his vocabulary.[10] A little more than a year before the Berlin Wall fell, the chancellor forecast he would not live to see it.[11] Later, with a politician's talent for flexible use of language, Kohl claimed he meant he would not live to see it as chancellor.[12]

Unreadiness for the adventure that lay ahead was a consequence of the accomplishment that had preceded it. West Germany established itself as the most stable and prosperous state in German history. Most Germans in the West had become accustomed to separation, and had grown comfortable with it. Division had brought West Germany not only costs but also benefits that would probably not have materialised had the nation remained united. As a consequence of the West's desire to make the rump state of West Germany a bulwark against communism, the Federal Republic attracted flows of aid and investment from the US that buttressed post-war recovery.[13] Membership of the European Community placed the country within a stable international framework. It gained markets for its exports, a central role in the rebuilding of the western part of the continent, and reconciliation with France, its old enemy from across the Rhine.[14]

After the infamy of Nazism, West Germany could concentrate on the objectives of recovery and western integration, two tasks that became fused into a single policy. Within their reduced borders, and subject to the continued (but barely onerous) loss of sovereignty stemming from continued four-power responsibility for 'Germany as a whole', the West Germans abandoned excessiveness and discovered efficiency. 'We are the trustees of the most infamous and fraudulent bankruptcy in history. We have practically only one choice – and that is work,' said Theodor Heuss, the Swabian journalist who in 1949 became West Germany's first president.[15] While West German politicians spread words of peace, industrialists scoured the world in search of export markets. As Edzard Reuter, chairman of Daimler–Benz from 1987 onwards, put it: 'The motto *exportare necesse est* was an important way of regaining international independence and respect after the ignominy of Hitler's atrocities.'[16] Most important of all, in the new objective of a united Europe, the Germans could proclaim an alternative, rather than an incitement, to the distractions of ideology and the intemperance of nationalism.

II

During the years of division, East Germany was not forgotten. Sometimes the loss of nationhood might cause dull pain; but restoring it slipped down the list of German priorities. Reflecting the bonds of history and culture, and the millions of shared recollections and family ties, many West Germans felt a vague sense of responsibility for their compatriots. But as they stilled their *Wanderlust* during foreign holidays, the West Germans became more at home in Paris than Potsdam, more familiar with Bangkok than Bautzen, happier to be in the Dominican

Republic than Dresden. Occasional pangs of guilt could be assuaged by the eastward dispatch of gifts and D-Marks at Christmas and birthdays, by a fulsome welcome extended to pallid eastern relatives on brief, officially tolerated visits across the divide. The western politicians who travelled to the East could enjoy the best of both worlds: the acclaim afforded to those who built bridges across the divided nation, and the relief invariably experienced when they arrived back safely on the western side.[10]

There was a strong feeling, in political parties, and among ordinary voters, that East Germany was an ugly, but necessary keystone in the post-war European mosaic. In a sentiment shared by many, Günter Peise, a Leipzig-born professor living in Münster in West Germany, summed up what appeared to be reality:

> I have experienced the pain of division. We were deprived of part of the nation. That left the people with a wound. The emotional links become less now as the family links die away. My son says I'm slightly mad to talk about it! We speak the same language as the people in the East, but we use it differently. We have different living standards. We can't proclaim that we will make Europe more stable through reunification. On the contrary: being divided is the price we pay for more stability.[18]

When ministers and officials in Bonn warned that a rebellion in East Germany could lead to Soviet military intervention,[19] similar to the outcome of the short-lived East German uprising in 1953, they were voicing the fear that, should this central element of Europe's post-war order be dislodged, the whole continent could face instability. Apprehension and yearning went hand in hand. Wolfgang Schäuble, the former interior minister, wheelchair-bound after an assassination attempt in 1990, who none the less became the conservative parties' Bundestag floor-leader in the early 1990s, stated in 1988: 'Reunification is not on the agenda at the moment – it would lead to instability and the danger of a neutralised Germany. But this division is so unnatural.'[20]

If, for many West German citizens, new-found stability made reunification difficult to contemplate, or even unthinkable, in the East, it made it irresistible. As soon as the shackles of Soviet imperialism started to loosen under the leadership of Mikhail Gorbachev, East Germans' anger, frustration and bitterness about the shortcomings of life under communism bubbled to the surface. These were emotions felt even (and sometimes particularly) by many former communists who had previously supported the regime; and they could be assuaged only by prompt accession to a prosperous and secure united Germany.

In 1989-90, the East Germans were seeking reparations for past misrule, mismanagement and misdeed: for the damage wrought by four decades of Soviet economic exploitation, for the break-up of families victimised by arbitrary judgement and punishment, for the state's systematic oppression of individuals who refused to obey its rules. What could be a more appropriate repository of hope than the neighbour who had profited rather than suffered from post-war cleavage? Who could better supply the compensation the East Germans desperately sought than the country that appeared, through its wealth, confidence and democracy, to be everything East Germany was not?

This act of national compensation was bound to exact

a price. When the hour of reunification arrived, not least because of the uneasy awareness that they would have to pay a large share of the bill, West Germans showed little evidence either of genuine national feeling or of the 'brotherly love' for their compatriots in the East postulated in 1955 by Chancellor Adenauer. Yet, equally, there was little understanding of the reality that, at least during the next few years, Germany would be poorer rather than wealthier. The heady atmosphere in which the East Germans suddenly gained freedom intensified their belief that, in the West, they would find succour. The West Germans were pleased, if also slightly disturbed, to be the focus of such hopes. Conscious of how the newly liberated states of central and eastern Europe saw in Germany a model on which to base their own progress towards free-market democracy, one of Kohl's closest aides asked in 1990, 'If we cannot make a success of unification, who is likely to succeed anywhere else?'[21] The Bonn government recognised that expectations were inflated, but it made inadequate efforts to reduce them to a more realistic level.

The gap between desire and feasibility was a measure of the gulf between Germany's ambitions and its resources. Yet in 1990 Kohl stubbornly refused to countenance decisive steps to finance unification through a large redistribution of national income. His rejection of tax increases reflected a mixture of insouciance about economic policy and, more important, instinctive knowledge of how to win elections.[22] In a year which saw the Germans go to the polls twice, first in March (in the election of the first democratic East German parliament) and in December (in the election of an all-German Bundestag), Kohl was challenged to raise taxes by Oskar Lafontaine, the Saarland prime minister and the Social Democrats' candidate for the chancellorship. He refused. Instead, Kohl proclaimed that, after a period of adjustment, reunification would virtually finance itself by generating additional tax receipts. He delivered a message that voters were both disinclined to believe yet relieved to hear.[23]

Kohl's pledge that 'no one will have to give up anything for German unity' was economically unsound. From a political point of view, however, ridiculing opposition contentions about the costs of unification gave Kohl an unparalleled opportunity to present his Christian Democrats as the party of national unity, and the Social Democrats as unpatriotic faint-hearts. Adenauer's celebrated dictum of 'No experiments', first coined in the 1957 general elections, was turned on its head. With a sensation of pride, exhilaration and anxiety, the country headed for an unforeseen trial.

The party bickering over the costs of unity indicated how Germany was running short of political consensus. It was also a harbinger of how reunited Germany would remain split in psychological and economic terms across the East–West divide. President Richard von Weizsäcker, a man who constantly showed greater sensitivity than Kohl over the problems of unification, stated that forty years of division could be overcome only by a better and fairer distribution of the country's resources.[24] Weizsäcker was, however, made uncomfortably aware during 1990 that his office wielded no real power to shape the course of unification. The imbalance in attitudes and emotions across the East–West German border, the greatest source of momentum behind unity, was set to become the greatest hurdle to its succe[ss] East Germans' eagerness to taste the fruits of th[e] was matched only by the West Germans' reluctance to share them.

III

Because of the unique sensitivities surrounding German unification, travelling towards it was like passing through a maze of distorting mirrors. No policy, no action, no statement, no objective could ever be taken completely at face value. During four decades, it was a journey in two directions at once. In the years after 1949, successive federal chancellors recognised that unification could be accomplished only if West Germany made maximum efforts to strengthen its economic, political and military ties to the European Community and Nato. Michael Stürmer, one of Germany's leading historians, laid down the leitmotif: 'The Federal Republic can never throw more weight into the scales of the East than it has in the scales of the West.'[25]

The war's aftermath not only placed the two parts of Germany under the ultimate juridical control of the victor nations, it also deposited a supreme black mark of historical disfavour against Germany's name. To restore it, and to contemplate re-establishing national sovereignty and territorial integrity, post-war Germany was required to establish its credentials as a reliable international partner. There was one other precondition. West Germany had also to become an eminently humble partner: subsuming its interests to those of the western alliance, eschewing independent use of military force, reassuring its allies that it saw its destiny in European rather than national terms, ostentatiously playing down the practical possibilities for reunification (sometimes, to a greater degree than foreign observers).[26] To reattain room for national manoeuvre, West Germany first had to place itself in a position where it appeared to have none.

The twin-track element of the strategy was encapsulated in a policy started tentatively under the 1966–69 Grand Coalition of Chancellor Kiesinger. It was provided with strength and strategic purpose by Willy Brandt when he became West Germany's first Social Democrat chancellor in 1969: building up political and economic ties with communist Europe, including the first steps towards recognising East Germany as a separate state. After the signing of treaties with the Soviet Union and Poland in 1970, diplomatic relations with East Germany were consummated with the signing of the Basic Treaty between the two Germanys in 1972.

West Germany's reasons for fostering ties with East Germany may certainly have included the belief that, if over the long term East Germany was to be undermined, it first had to be stabilised. In 1963 Egon Bahr, one of the architects of Brandt's *Ostpolitik*, outlined the thesis of *Wandel durch Annäherung* (change through rapprochement): division could be overcome not by confrontation but through cooperation.

By underpinning East Germany's short-term future, West Germany could plausibly argue that it was contributing in two different ways to the long-term aim of ending the separation of the two German states. First, Bonn was providing the East German authorities with the self-confidence to implement genuine reforms – a route which might eventually lead to unification if a democratically elected East Berlin government came to power. Second, any action to lower tension along the East–West German border would help foster an improvement in the overall climate of East–West *détente*, a crucial condition for overcoming division with the East. Intriguingly, the Soviet Union seems to have enjoyed insight into the purpose of West Germany's strategy. Referring to Brandt's *Ostpolitik* overtures, Soviet leader Leonid Brezhnev told Erich Honecker in 1970 (a year before the latter took over the leadership of the East German communist party from Walter Ulbricht), 'He expects to penetrate you . . . But with time he will find that even harder.'[27]

The stabilisation of East Germany was implemented from the 1970s onwards through political and economic means. East Germany was recognised as a separate state (though not as a separate nation). After the signing of the Basic Treaty, the two Germanys entered the United Nations as separate members in 1973. West Germany channelled eastwards a wide variety of financial assistance, estimated at 7 to 10 per cent of the communist state's annual economic output, with the cash devoted to purposes ranging from repairing road and rail links to restoring churches.[28] After unification in 1990, transfers increased to an amount equivalent to more than 50 per cent of East Germany's output as measured by gross domestic product: one striking sign of constancy in German economic life.

An important component of the aid, given little public attention before 1989, stemmed from the Bonn government's policy of buying political prisoners' freedom from East German jails.[29] A practice that was conceived in the early 1960s as a palliative for East Germany's summary imprisonment of dissidents became embedded in the state's system of centralised planning. As one of the leading West German officials involved in the exchanges admitted: 'We give money, the GDR gives people.'[30] By providing a financial inducement for the release and exile of those who had fallen foul of the police state, the system not only gave East Berlin a regular source of much-needed foreign currency, but also lowered internal pressure for genuine change. Many independent-minded East Germans, who after spells in jail, would otherwise have swollen the opposition movement, achieved their freedom – but found themselves on the western side of the Elbe. The ransoming of prisoners was one of the reasons why East Germany, in contrast to other members of the Soviet bloc, found itself virtually bereft of leaders after the collapse of communism.

West Germany's right-wing parties had hotly opposed Brandt's *Ostpolitik* on the grounds that it abandoned German national interests. None the less, when Kohl's Christian Democrat-led coalition came to power in 1982, it effectively continued the policies towards the East developed under Brandt and his successor Helmut Schmidt, who had taken over in 1974. The policies of government and opposition were, however, marked by one important difference. Despite suggestions during the 1980s from parts of the SPD, the Kohl government refused to submit to the oft-repeated East German demand that it recognise separate East German citizenship. Had it done so, the East Germans who, since the country's foundation in 1949, had sought to flee to the West would have been treated as foreigners when they arrived in West Germany. The process of unification sparked by outflows of discontented easterners in 1989-90 would then have taken a different course.

Without the progress in western integration and, in particular, without the overriding safeguard of a strong military link with the US, *Ostpolitik* as practised by Brandt and his successors would not have been possible. Yet there was a drawback. As the cement holding in place the superpower blocs of East and West appeared to harden, the *Westpolitik* of integrating Germany firmly with the West, rather than bringing reunification closer as Adenauer had asserted, appeared to place ever larger barriers in front of it. In 1988, Bahr wrote that the European Community's planned move at the end of 1992 to a 'single market' – a Europe-wide unified trade zone – made unification impossible, as it would irreversibly lock the Federal Republic to the West. He called for the two German states at last to sign the delayed post-war peace treaties that would confirm their existence as separate states, but would also give the Germans the freedom to decide their own destiny as a reunited nation.[31]

Bahr's basic premise that unification could take place only if West Germany were detached from the EC and Nato proved faulty.[32] The evident hollowness of this thesis contributed to the overall discrediting of the SPD's policies towards East Germany – an important factor in both the 1990 and the 1994 general election campaigns. The conclusion that membership of the European Community and Nato might prove inimical to reunification was also, however, drawn by some Christian Democrats, as well as by the far Right political groupings who by the end of the 1980s started to attract significant electoral support for the first time in twenty years.[33]

Sporadic signs of impatience from Left and Right about the official policy of stabilising East–West German ties were hardly representative of West German public opinion as a whole. But they highlighted the seeming permanence of the post-war structure and of the policies upholding it. When Honecker paid a long-delayed official visit to Bonn in 1987, he was greeted with military honours and the ceremonial flying of the two separate German flags in Kohl's headquarters at the *Bundeskanzleramt*. The chancellor paid his respects to his eastern guest through gritted teeth, but in his speech at the official banquet treated his visitor to only a mild-mannered reprimand about shootings at the Berlin Wall. The two sides signed a variety of cooperation agreements; they discussed improvements in tourism and town planning; and the chancellor was in sufficiently convivial mood to swap reminiscences with Honecker about their common acquaintances from south-west Germany.[34] Reunification had demonstrably been laid to rest as an operational objective of Bonn policy. Only three years before its demise, the German Democratic Republic appeared to have come of age.

IV

If West Germany's original aspiration had been that financial, technological and economic assistance would give East Germany's rulers the self-assurance and flexibility to agree democratic reforms, then, by the 1980s, the plan seemed to have misfired. Help from the West increased material living standards and encouraged the East German leadership – sometimes as a result of specific West German bargaining [35] – to relax constraints on contacts between East and West. However, the policy of ideological separation – *Abgrenzung* or 'fencing off' – launched by Honecker when he became party leader in 1971 became ever more rigid: a cage of East Germany's own making. The country's constitution was revised in 1974 to delete the earlier reference to the 'German nation' and to redefine the German Democratic Republic as 'a socialist state of workers and farmers' indissolubly linked to the Soviet Union. During the 1970s and 1980s, the state strengthened direction of the *Kombinate*, the centrally organised industrial enterprises. The police and security services maintained tight control over would-be dissidents. The East–West gulf seemed to have become permanent.

East Germany's reluctance to espouse the principles of liberal capitalism gained ground for three principal reasons. First, at a time when East Germany's relative economic performance was faltering, each D-Mark flowing across the Elbe enlarged East Germany's dependence on the West – and thus its sense of vulnerability. That insecurity was increased by the manifest evidence that East Germany was neither a state in which its citizens felt comfortable nor one to which they felt loyalty. Between its establishment in 1949 and the building of the Berlin Wall in 1961, 2.69 million East Germans fled to the West – one-fifth of its original population. During the twenty-seven years up to the end of 1988, 616,000 crossed westwards, some of them braving death on the fortified border. A tidal wave of 344,000 came across in 1989, and 192,000 followed in the first six months of 1990 before the streams at last began to ebb with the prospect of political unification.

Second, the East German authorities' opposition to reforms was heightened by the perception, more acute in East Berlin than in Bonn, that a reformed version of East German communism would inevitably open the door to reunification. The clearest exposition came from Otto Reinhold, one of East Germany's principal party ideologists, in 1989. 'The German Democratic Republic is conceivable only as an anti-fascist, socialist state, as a socialist alternative to the Federal Republic . . . What right of existence should a capitalist East Germany have next to a capitalist Federal Republic? Naturally, none.'[36]

Third, Mikhail Gorbachev's attempts to restructure Soviet communism exposed East Germany to new pressure on its eastern flank to adjust its political and economic structures – intensifying the Honecker regime's fear and obduracy.[37] In a masterly misrepresentation of reality, Honecker described East Germany's economic planning system as 'efficient, dynamic and flexible'.[38] Turning to one of the exaggeratedly homely metaphors that the Germans often deploy to depict epoch-breaking events, Kurt Hager, the SED's veteran ideologist, dismissed Gorbachev's attempts to restructure the Soviet system as akin to 'changing the wallpaper' in a neighbouring apartment.[39] The gerontocratic leadership in East Berlin wanted to hide the truth not only from the outside world, but also from itself.

The old men were struggling against mounting odds. As a result of the much-increased opportunity to pay short-term visits to the West, large numbers of ordinary East Germans had gained direct experience of West Germany – increasing their frustrations with the shabby immobility of life under Honecker. Reflecting the superficial nature of these visits and the influence of West German television watched on the other side of the Elbe, many East Germans undoubtedly built up an unrealistically high opinion of West German living standards. This could only amplify the impetus for change.

The economic pressures, too, were intensifying. Rising foreign currency debts led to increasing pessimism among the regime's own economic experts. A document drawn up in September 1989 by a group of advisers to the East German Politburo, which came to light in 1992, spelled out the sobering truth: East Germany was 'to the widest extent dependent on capitalist credit'. To allow the country to maintain payments on its foreign currency liabilities, the experts urged thoroughgoing action to hold back domestic consumption and double exports to the West during the next five years.[40]

Potent new factors were introduced into the German equation by the changing nature of the superpower relationship and the course of nuclear disarmament negotiations in 1988-89. By the end of the 1980s, as part of the *détente* engendered by Gorbachev's conciliatory foreign policies, the US and the Soviet Union were preparing to bargain away all their medium-range nuclear missiles (of more than 500 kilometre range) stationed in Europe. The Germans on both sides of the Elbe were strongly in favour of removing nuclear arms. But they were uncomfortably aware that, once the agreement had been implemented to remove all missiles with a range of more than 500 kilometres, the only nuclear missiles left in Europe would be short-range weapons stationed in Germany and Czechoslovakia. If used, by definition, they could explode across a region of central Europe largely defined by the territory of East and West Germany.

This realisation had an important impact on the German collective psyche – bringing to the fore a previously quiescent sense of solidarity across the Elbe. No one was more sensitive to the new climate than Hans-Dietrich Genscher, the West German foreign minister with his roots in Halle in East Germany. Although he had maintained active links with his homeland throughout his political career, since the 1960s he had progressively lost hope of German unification. As the disarmament talks progressed in 1989, he was one of the first politicians to realise that the reunification issue might find its way back on the German political agenda. In a memorable speech to the Bundestag in April 1989, he pointed out that the residual nuclear weapons were designed to explode in 'the other part of our Fatherland.' Combatting these weapons' deadly potential, he suggested, provided a test of whether the Germans would live up to their responsibilities for the entire German nation.[41] For the first time, a significant defence policy gap between West Germany's interests and those of its Nato allies started to emerge. The ticking of the clock was barely perceptible, yet the countdown to unification had begun.

The tide turning against East Germany was increasing in strength. In view of the dramatic changes in outside circumstances in 1989-90, with hindsight it appears certain that even the most far-reaching reforms would not have preserved East Germany as a separate state. In fact, East Berlin refused to take any action to adapt to the unfavourable international environment. Fed by intransigence and inflexibility, the forces for change became overwhelming.

The East Berlin regime had appeared to leave nothing to chance. One of its supreme contradictions, however, was that it had formulated no plans for its own renewal. During the summer and autumn of 1989, the exodus of dissatisfied East Germans to the Federal Republic had increased sharply, with many of them arriving via Hungary – which opened its border with Austria in May 1989 – and Czechoslovakia. Gorbachev's message that each member of the Soviet bloc had to find its own path to non-violent reform provided a strong hint to ordinary East Germans that the Red Army would not intervene to maintain East German order. Once other countries in the Soviet bloc opened their frontiers, there was no way, short of building a wall around East Germany, that

the country could control the problem that had sapped
its legitimacy since its inception: the constant seepage
of its population towards the land of freedom and the
D-Mark. East Germany subsided as sand succumbs to a
running sea.

The end came in a sudden swirl of events that
combined high emotion with strong traces of farce. On
9 November 1989, it seems reasonably certain that East
Germany had no intention of opening the Berlin Wall.[42]
At 7 p.m., when Günter Schabowski, the Politburo
member responsible for press and information matters,
announced new regulations to simplify application procedures for exit visas, the step was intended as nothing
more than a stop-gap measure to lower the surge of
illegal emigration. Misunderstanding (perhaps wilfully)
Schabowski's confusingly worded statement, crowds
gathered at the Wall demanding the right to cross
to West Berlin without visas. The border guards were
unsure of their instructions, but they sensed that the
old order – in Germany and in Europe – had run its
course. Over the decades, East Germany's lifeblood had
grown ever thinner. As the sentinels allowed the excited
and uncertain multitudes to pass, they watched it drain
away.

V

German unification could never be a matter solely for
the Germans. This was not simply because the outcome
of the war in 1945 had made the victors legally and
politically responsible for the nation's destiny. In Germany, more than anywhere else in Europe and perhaps
the world, foreign attitudes have a direct impact on

the population's view of itself – a factor which critically affected the path to unity. As the drive towards political unification accelerated, it seemed evident to many West Germans that the recombined parts of the nation would form Europe's economic superpower. They could be excused for holding this view, since it was proclaimed with varying degrees of vigour by most of West Germany's partners and neighbours.[43]

In a formal sense, political support for unification had long since been pledged by the western allies. The US, Britain and France, signatories along with West Germany of the Bonn Convention (*Deutschlandvertrag*), a treaty that came into effect in 1955, undertook to work for a unified Germany that would be 'integrated into the European community' and possess a 'liberal-democratic constitution'.[44] However, until the chance of unity actually arose, many in Germany surmised that this promise might amount to little more than empty words. As Alfred Grosser, one of France's leading specialists on Franco-German relations, wrote, the allies were suspected of giving support to reunification only when it was not possible.[45] The upheavals of 1989–90 provided an opportunity to test whether or not this cynical view was correct. For Britain and France, it turned out that it was.

Margaret Thatcher, the British prime minister, was quickly identified as the West's most implacable opponent of rapid unification. She had few qualms in admitting that the post-war pro-unification pledges were not to be taken seriously. In September 1989, two months before the Berlin Wall fell, as the flood of departing East Germans brought the theme of reunification back into newspaper headlines for the first time for a generation, Thatcher made a brief visit to Moscow.

She later summed up her message to Gorbachev: 'Although Nato had traditionally made statements supporting Germany's aspiration to be reunited, in practice we were rather apprehensive.'[46]

Thatcher's desire to slow down unification was, she claimed, based partly on the belief that it would undermine Gorbachev and set back *détente*. However, her statements in 1989–90 made it clear that her overriding reason was the fear that a united Germany would be 'stronger than all others'[47] and 'a very dominant nation'.[48] Thatcher was even worried that the Germans would start to have large families again. Failing to foresee the effect of reunification in reducing still further the chronically low German birth rate, she believed that, if reunified, Germany's population growth would destabilise its neighbours.[49]

Thatcher was one of the few world leaders whose public statements on German unification appeared to be in full accord with views held in private. She was not averse to using ceremonial occasions to make known her opinions about German history. At a formal dinner at the annual Anglo-German Königswinter conference in 1990, celebrating forty years of Anglo-German friendship, she told one astonished German ex-ambassador: 'You need another forty years before we can forget what you have done.'[50] Her candour in refusing to hide her feelings behind diplomatic subterfuge both irritated Kohl and won his grudging respect.[51] They had little in common save their affiliation to right-wing parties.

Thatcher's visit to Kohl's home region of Rhineland-Palatinate in April 1989 offered several revealing examples of their capacity for mutual misunderstanding.[52] At the welcoming ceremony, Thatcher spoke of her great pleasure at being in France.[53] She used most of the visit to lecture Kohl on the importance of modernising short-range nuclear missiles stationed in Germany – a course to which the chancellor was ill-disposed. During a brief tour of nearby Speyer cathedral, Kohl confided to Thatcher's private secretary, Charles Powell, that he wanted to show her he was 'as much European as German.' His gesture failed to make an impact. During the flight back to London, the prime minister exclaimed: 'Isn't he [Kohl] so German!'[54]

Thatcher's hostility to reunification exaggerated the true level of concern felt by the British people.[55] However, she acted as a focus for the sentiment, widely held in Europe, that the Germans could still not be trusted. A surreal debate on Germany at Chequers in March 1990 between the prime minister and half a dozen academic experts came to the conclusion – according to Powell's resumé of the meeting, subsequently leaked to the press – that the Germans were prone to 'angst, aggressiveness, assertiveness, bullying, egotism, inferiority complex, sentimentality.'[56] Powell believes Thatcher's views on Germany owe much to childhood memories of wartime Middle England: 'She had long-term worries about the consequences of German unity and how best to handle it. For a small girl growing up in Grantham, the Germans were about as evil as anything you could think of.' A man highly sympathetic to Thatcher and with a strong understanding of her sensibilities, Powell put forward a devastatingly simple explanation for the former prime minister's anti-German feeling. It had less to do with Realpolitik than with envy at Germany's post-war recovery.[57]

France demonstrated a different kind of sensitivity. In view of the country's threefold experience of German invasion since 1870, the concerns went deeper and wider. But they were expressed more subtly, and they were linked to a commitment to counter the risks of unification through a policy of 'binding' Germany to a more integrated Europe. If this was a special relationship, it was also delicate and many-layered. Founding fathers of the European Community, partners in bilateral cooperation after the signing of the Elysée Treaty in 1963, France and West Germany had become joint pursuers of the holy grail of European unity. President François Mitterrand and Chancellor Kohl had inherited the spirit and the mantle of Charles de Gaulle and Konrad Adenauer.

There was, however, another side to the relationship geared less to trust than to foreboding. Throughout the post-war period, Bonn needed to demonstrate, and Paris needed to be told, that Germany would no longer be a danger to European stability. The greater Germany's power, either real or perceived, the more pressing would be France's requirement for reasssurance.

It was clear that the ending of German division would have deep consequences for France. Outwardly, Mitterrand's public performance was relaxed. In November 1989 – less than a week before the Wall fell – he was the first western leader publicly to forecast German reunification; he said he was 'not afraid' of it.[58] Subsequently, it was claimed that Mitterrand foresaw as early as 1981 that a coming collapse of the Soviet empire made German reunification inevitable within a generation.[59] In reality, Mitterrand was less composed and confident than such remarks might have suggested.[60] The French goverment's private anxieties over the prospects of German unity appear to have been comparable with those outlined in public by Margaret Thatcher.[61]

Concerned like the British prime minister that German

unification could destabilise Gorbachev, Mitterrand flew to Kiev in December 1989 to discuss Germany's future with the Soviet president. According to one semi-authoritative French account, Gorbachev made an impassioned plea for French help in avoiding unification.[62] This visit, along with Mitterrand's hastily arranged journey to East Berlin later that month, strengthened the impression in Bonn that France wished to preserve for as long as possible the old constellation of European power.[63]

French worries about German unpredictability were increased by Kohl's delay in confirming the inviolability of Poland's western border, fixed in 1945 after Polish annexation of German territory east of the Oder–Neisse rivers – an action which had never been upheld in international law. Pressed by domestic right-wingers agitating for the reintegration of the 'eastern territories', Kohl maintained unnecessary ambiguity about whether a united Germany would seek to renegotiate its eastern border with Poland. He waited until March 1990 before stating formally that Germany had no claims on the former German lands in the East. Horst Teltschik, Kohl's foreign affairs adviser and one of his main experts on relations with East Germany, recorded that France's insistence on clarifying the Polish question was one more sign that France wanted to 'slow down' reunification. 'Mistrust of the Germans,' he concluded, 'runs deep.'[64]

VI

Perspectives on Germany depend on the vantage point of the beholder. At a distance of 4,000 miles, the government in Washington felt able to proclaim support for the German people's right to freedom and self-determination with considerably greater conviction than that exhibited in Paris or London.[65] President Ronald Reagan's policies encouraged Moscow to struggle in vain to match America's arms spending efforts. This greatly contributed to the ebbing of Soviet power that made reunification possible. In the years afterwards, Kohl and his advisers contrasted the consistent backing for unification shown by Reagan's successor George Bush with the hesitancy displayed by Mitterrand and Thatcher.[66] During the war with Iraq which broke out in January 1991, Germany made some recompense for America's unification support by giving important logistical help in the airlifting of men and equipment to the Gulf.

Two years earlier, at the beginning of 1989, US–German ties had been severely strained by American revelations that German companies had helped equip a chemical weapons factory in Libya, viewed by the US as a potential threat to Israel. However, by the time Bush made a state visit to West Germany in May 1989, relations had greatly improved, helped by US understanding for Kohl's desire to avoid a new round of nuclear armament. Eschewing the hectoring tones adopted by Thatcher, Bush realised that pressing the Germans towards a decision on modernising short-range US missiles in Germany would be counterproductive. He quickly grasped a basic condition for winning influence in Bonn: the Germans like not only to be taken seriously, but also to be liked. During his May 1989 visit, Bush took care to emphasise the country's pivotal position in Europe, terming the Germans 'partners in leadership.' This description, although partly a successful attempt to flatter Kohl, gave a real indication of changing US priorities. The traditional 'special relationship' with Britain was becoming less special. After the end of the Cold War, American and German destinies remained linked in one important respect. Both countries – the world's sole superpower, and the largest economy in Europe – were the focus of inflated foreign policy expectations. Both failed to live up to them.

Although the US displayed conspicuously greater sure-footedness during the unification drama than that shown by either Britain or France, several episodes revealed marked differences on the issue within the Bush administration. With unusual directness and prescience, Vernon Walters, the veteran US soldier-diplomat who became ambassador to Bonn in April 1989, stated several times in the first few months after his arrival that reunification would soon be on the diplomatic agenda.[67] These statements earned him a series of rebukes from James Baker, the US secretary of state. Like Genscher, the West German foreign minister, Baker wanted to take a gradual approach to unification that would not provoke fears in Britain, France and, above all, the Soviet Union about upheaval in the centre of Europe.[69]

The Americans showed sporadic anxiety, like the British and French, that Germany would 'purchase' its unity from the Soviet Union by agreeing to depart from Nato. For the Chancellor, this was a matter on which he could afford no hint of wavering. He gave considerably greater priority to calming US worries over Nato membership than to quietening French vexation over the Polish border. Kohl assured Bush in early 1990 that united Germany would remain in the Atlantic alliance. There was, however, a strong body of opinion in Washington that events could turn out otherwise. An internal US intelligence report in 1990 postulated that a united Germany would most likely withdraw from Nato.[70] Writing in 1994, Robert Blackwill, a top US official active in the 1990 Bush-Kohl exchanges, contrasted the American line with the suspicion shown towards Germany by Britain and France: 'We trusted Kohl.' He added, 'In insisting on full Nato membership for united Germany, Bush and Kohl were swimming against a strong tide generated by sceptical western experts in and out of government.'[71]

The US recognised the important hold over large sections of German public opinion enjoyed by Mikhail Gorbachev. What was not realised, however, was the effect that German unification would have on Gorbachev's own fate. No foreign leader stood to gain or lose more from German unity than the Soviet president. East Germany had been the Soviet Union's principal prize of the Second World War. If it slipped out of Moscow's grip, this could clearly lower further Gorbachev's domestic popularity, jeopardising chances of bringing to fruition his increasingly problematic reforms. If, as a condition for unification, Moscow could detach the Federal Republic from the western sphere of influence, this could rank as an important foreign policy success. On the other hand, the Soviet Union – like the West – had a clear interest in choosing an international political framework for a united Germany that would improve the country's prospects of stability. Without stability in Germany, Gorbachev wrote in 1987, 'There would be no hope for stability in Europe, and hence for the world.'[72]

This was one Gorbachev dictum which did not change over time. In other pronunciations of policy towards Germany, Gorbachev was forced by circumstances to change his mind. Up to and after November 1989, Gorbachev maintained the communist party's strong traditional opposition to German unity. He warned Kohl in Moscow in October 1988 that trying to overturn division, which he termed 'the outcome of history', would be 'an incalculable and even dangerous undertaking'.[73] To support his contention, Gorbachev turned to Goethe: 'For new truths, nothing is as dangerous as old errors.' The Soviet president repeated his distaste for unification to Thatcher in Moscow in September 1989.[74] Next month, during the ceremonies in East Berlin to commemorate East Germany's fortieth anniversary, Gorbachev repeated that attempts to overcome German division could threaten stability across Europe[75] – reinforcing a message to which he knew that the French and British governments were particularly susceptible. When he saw Mitterrand in Kiev in December 1989, Gorbachev played on the French president's own anxieties by telling him that unification could lead not only to the 'militarisation' of the Moscow government but also to 'war on the continent'.[76]

Important forces were thus arrayed against rapid German unification: the Soviet Union and, to a lesser extent, Britain and France – three of the five permanent members of the United Nations security council. The course of German unity was, however, being decided not in the chancelleries of London, Bonn or Moscow, but on the streets of Suhl, Cottbus and Rostock. In February 1990, when he sensed there was no practical method of holding it up, Gorbachev signalled his agreement to reunification in a historic declaration with Kohl in Moscow. Later, at a further meeting with Kohl in the Caucasus in July 1990, Gorbachev gave his blessing to the crucial condition that a united Germany would be part of Nato.

Gorbachev's own source of compensation was the likelihood that Germany's financial and industrial power could be turned to Moscow's advantage. The groundwork for persuading him that unification might benefit the Soviet Union had been laid during a conversation with Kohl on Gorbachev's first visit to Bonn in June 1989, in the grounds of the chancellor's office by the Rhine.[77] When Gorbachev next visited Bonn in November 1990 – exactly a year after the Wall fell – Germany had been united for a month. In marked contrast to his remarks in Moscow in 1988, the Soviet leader proclaimed: 'The new vision of the world has triumphed.' Again he turned for poetic inspiration to Goethe, but in a markedly different sense from the one he had outlined two years ago: 'Humanity holds sway over every nation.'[78]

East Germany's defection from the communist camp started a chain reaction that was to lead, more quickly than anyone had surmised, to the logical conclusion of the dismantling of Stalinism: the disintegration of the Soviet empire. As Kohl had hinted to Gorbachev in 1989, united Germany was likely to prove a valuable economic and political partner for the East on a redrawn map of Europe. Neither Kohl nor Gorbachev foresaw that the Soviet Union would no longer be on it.

VII

During the first few months of unity, the incipient break-up of the Soviet Union added to the uncertainties facing the new Germany. The euphoria that had greeted the fall of the Berlin Wall persisted only a few months east of the Elbe; in the West, it lasted only a few weeks. On German Unity Day, on 3 October 1990, the pessimists declared it would take a generation to integrate the two parts of the nation. By the following year, even the optimists knew this judgement was correct.

Post-war West Germany had been formed and defined by geographical, political and economic constraints. These became less binding; the area that they enclosed, more amorphous. West Germany's legal code, democracy, economic system, currency and place in the European Community and Nato were all extended eastwards, as were its politicians, banks, automobiles, consumer goods, and advertising slogans. Exporting West Germany's successful trappings, however, guaranteed neither that success itself would be transferred, nor that it was even transferable.

There was a national consensus in favour of unification. Yet once the treaties and agreements, internal and external, had been negotiated and signed, there was insufficient accord on how to guide the process through to fruition. There was general agreement that the East Germans who, even after 9 November 1989, were continuing to stream westwards in search of a better life, should be awarded compensation for forty years of hardship. But there was no general readiness in the West to make sacrifices to fulfil this goal. There was awareness that the new Germany would not simply be the old Federal Republic with its population increased by one-quarter. But what sort of nation would it be?

One clue was provided by the circumstances of the entry of the D-Mark into East Germany, decided in February 1990 and implemented in July. This was a decisive step along the road to full-scale unification. If this was a revolution, however, the driving force was not new-found national fervour, but fear of mass migration and the disruption it would bring.

On one level, German monetary union was a bold

step to use Germany's strongest asset – its currency – to weld together the two parts of the nation.[79] Kohl was justifiably concerned to exploit the opportunity of a favourable political climate in the Soviet Union to build an unshakeable economic bridge between the two Germanys. As the chancellor put it, in perhaps the best example of his penchant for naturalistic metaphor, 'We must gather in the hay before the storm.'[80] The July introduction of the D-Mark was no mere technical exercise. As a result, East Germany gave up any question of running an independent economic policy, starting the countdown to full political unification three months later.

On the other hand, however, the D-Mark move was a defensive measure to forestall the possibility that hundreds of thousands of dissatisfied East Germans would travel westwards and dislocate West Germany's well-ordered society. In early 1990, the easterners were not pursuing freedom. Following the collapse of the communist regime, that was already making its arrival. They wanted economic security and higher living standards, and they wanted to avoid, if they could, the unsettling effect of capitalism as it crossed the Elbe.

With the conviction of a born optimist, Kohl forecast that the ambitious young people of East Germany would provide 'enlivening competition' for the West.[81] Yet competition for jobs, homes and social security in West Germany was not what the chancellor had in mind. Reunification of the German people on West German soil was a form of national unity that had to be avoided at all costs.

The advent of the D-Mark in East Germany was heralded as a repetition of the successful currency reform of June 1948 in the western zones of occupied

The Melting of the Ice

Germany. The replacement of the worthless Reichsmark by the Deutsche Mark was coupled with the abolition of price controls by Ludwig Erhard, the economics director of the US and British zones. He later became West Germany's first economics minister between 1949 and 1963, a time of great economic buoyancy. By providing a solid currency to lubricate West Germany's seized-up economic machine, the 1948 measures paved the way for Erhard's 'social market economy' and the era of the *Wirtschaftswunder* (economic miracle).

The 1990 currency conversion, by contrast, launched a voyage into an economic void. The high exchange rate chosen for the East Mark – which was worth at most only 20 pfennigs (and sometimes a lot less) on the black market – satisfied the desires of East German consumers. But it subjected East German industry to a currency revaluation of 400 per cent, making East German goods colossally over-priced by comparison with competitors from West Germany and abroad. The monetary conversion exposed the full frailty of East Germany's outdated, underinvested and overmanned industrial system. It led to massive unemployment, and to further East German migration to West Germany: a land that still exerted a strong magnetic attraction, above all because it remained, after unification, very different from the East.

VIII

Like most forms of the German nation throughout history, the new Germany created on 3 October 1990 was an amalgam of disparate states. In past centuries, the patchwork of nationhood threaded together by stratagem, bribes or tyranny tended to tear under strain. In 1990, the fabric was a great deal more resistant, strengthened by democracy and the D-Mark. None the less, the danger of political fragmentation could not be overlooked as the Germans weathered a sudden surfeit of change.

In the East, even most people without jobs were better off in material terms – thanks to West German social security benefits – than they had been before when employed. Yet the evident inequality in the distribution of new wealth increased the potential for jealousy and ill will. Knowing how much they had previously been exploited, the population feared exploitation anew. The *Anschluss* to the Federal Republic had been eminently peaceful. But knowledge that their salvation and their future largely depended on institutions, laws and capital imported from the West increased neither the easterners' confidence nor their self-esteem; nor did the accelerated process of transition give them time to examine and digest the lessons of their past. Theodor Heuss, West Germany's first president, describing how his compatriots after the Second World War had paradoxically found their freedom under Allied occupation, termed them as having been 'rescued and destroyed at the same time'.[82] The post-Cold War East Germans, released from division yet trapped by new resentment, were in a not dissimilar position.

The Germans east of the Elbe were passing to a new life that most had profoundly desired. The world they were entering was a better one, but they did not feel it was their own. One East German doctor in 1991 described the 'spruce and well-combed' West Germans as the new occupying powers.[83] The easterners had prepared themselves for an economic boom, and it had failed to arrive, either in East Germany or across the liberated region of central and eastern Europe. Wolfgang Pohl, the mayor of Frankfurt an der Oder near the Polish border, commented: 'In the West, we have recession. In the East, the markets are not yet there.'[84] An industrialist, Klaus-Dieter Bilkenroth, chief executive of the Mitteldeutsche Bergbau lignite works in Bitterfeld, put it more graphically: 'We have experienced not restructuring but collapse.'[85]

The upheaval was bound to have political consequences. 'In East Germany, democracy has failed to put down roots,' concluded Elisabeth Noelle-Neumann of the Allensbach Institute, the doyenne of German opinion pollsters, in 1993. Confronted with large-scale unemployment and dashed hopes of rapidly catching up with West German living standards, 57 per cent of East Germans hankered after an improved form of the old communist system, according to a 1993 opinion poll.[86]

The opening of Europe's borders brought opportunities as well as strife. Economic competition and inflows of immigrants both increased, as did internationally organised crime. Additional support for far Right parties, attacks on foreigners by skinhead thugs,[87] and a general mood of disillusionment with established political parties, brought back, for some, memories of the Weimar Republic that traditionally resurface whenever Germany undergoes crisis.[88] There were frequent reminders, some of them ugly, of a resurgence of simple-minded nationalism. The Israeli author Amos Elon, describing a scene in 1992 in the market-place of Halle in East Germany, wrote:

I had the feeling of being inside a time machine, transported to the twenties. Some two hundred youths with shaven heads or Hitler hairdos and wearing black leather jackets and belts marked SS and black boots were standing in the square, screaming *'Sieg Heil'* and *'Ausländer Raus'* (foreigners out) as they held their right arms in the old Nazi salute. A girl with dyed blonde hair made into a thick braid was handling out leaflets honouring Rudolf Hess . . . A few young men were waving old imperial war flags (swastikas are illegal in Germany) . . . Trailed by a long caravan of police trucks – a helicopter kept roaring overhead – they marched off towards the university.[89]

Would the challenges heal or tear open lesions in German society? Would they create a new equilibrium in Europe or simply destroy the old one? Ever since Germany's nineteenth century unification, it had experienced greater oscillations than any other industrial nation. After 1945, fears of new crises, coupled with persistent memories of old ones, helped keep Germany peaceful and prosperous. As Europe cast off the post-war order amid both joy and apprehension, Germany faced a new task: to use the crisis of unity as an opportunity to renew itself and the continent around it. Unification was made possible by West Germany's stability and prosperity over forty years. During the aftermath, precisely those achievements were at risk.

A Difficult Transplant

As the first step, a currency reordering in the Soviet zone, through an inclusion in our monetary system, will be imperative. Inevitably, prices and wages will be aligned with those in the Federal Republic . . . Naturally, this process will ruthlessly expose the economic position of the Soviet zone, and the result will be distressing, if not shocking. We will have to reckon with a large gap in economic performance between East and West, with serious consequences for social conditions.

Ludwig Erhard, West German Economics Minister,
on prospects for German reunification, 1953[1]

In truth, everyone will profit from the future economic dynamics of East Germany . . . When could the Germans ever hope better to master the economic problems of unity than now, when everyone can see the German economy is in such outstanding form?

Helmut Kohl, West German Chancellor, 1990[2]

An avalanche has broken over me.

Hans-Joachim Maaz, East German psychotherapist,
on the psychological aftermath of unification, 1991[3]

I

Converting East Germany to capitalism is a uniquely complex operation. When the West Germans took stock of the task in 1990, they knew they were approaching uncharted territory. 'We know how to carry out heart transplants, kidney transplants, liver transplants. But here, we are changing all the organs at once,' said Gerhard Fels, director of the Institut der deutschen Wirtschaft, a Cologne-based economic research body financed by the Federation of German Industry (BDI).[4]

For the takeover of the East, the West German government launched an audacious prospectus. In 1990, Chancellor Kohl told the Germans in the East that the economic benefits of unification would become apparent relatively quickly, and he promised Germans in the West that these advantages could be generated without additional taxes. However, the promise that the fruits of reunification would soon be harvested proved irredeemable. The economic aftermath of unification became a vicious rather than a virtuous circle. Anxiety, not confidence, fed upon itself.

In 1990, the German government believed unification would lead to a self-perpetuating spiral of improving performance: the economic equivalent of channelling water uphill. The costs of unity would be defrayed by steadily increasing tax revenue as growth accelerated in East and West. 'I firmly reject any question of tax rises or emergency levies for East Germany,' stated Theo Waigel, Kohl's finance minister, in December 1989.[5] Waigel, a perennially hopeful Swabian who took over the post in April 1989, was one of Kohl's main cabinet allies in his position as head of the Christian Democrats' Bavarian sister party, the Christian Social Union. Waigel's statement at the end of 1989 formed the opening lines in a long litany of insouciance. 'For this enormous challenge, a limited rise in our borrowing is acceptable,' he said in February 1990.[6] During the summer, Waigel proclaimed: 'As the result of a brilliant economic outlook up to 1993, we will have extra tax revenues of DM115 billion.'[7]

The string of bravura predictions extended into 1991: 'In a few years' time, no one will speak any more about the financing and tax problems that occupy us so urgently today.'[8]

Although he held office in a period when fiscal overshooting was the international norm, Waigel's budgetary plans went awry to an extent unmatched anywhere else in Europe. The sole parallel was the failure of President Ronald Reagan to bring about planned deficit cuts in the US in the early 1980s. In both cases, reality displayed grim triumph over wishful thinking. For four successive years in Germany, planned reductions in fiscal deficits failed to materialise.[9] Underlining Waigel's lack of prescience, federal budget spending in 1994 was roughly DM60 billion higher than he had predicted only three years previously.[10]

As for the chancellor, he upheld the message that economic unification could be completed relatively quickly and without too much pain. 'In a few years, in three or four years, we will see a flourishing landscape in Thuringia, in Saxony-Anhalt, in Saxony, in Mecklenburg, in western Pomerania, in Brandenburg,' Kohl said in June 1990.[11] Although the people in the East faced a 'time of transition [that will] certainly not be easy,' he forecast in July 1990, the month of German monetary union, 'no one will be worse off.'[12] The government maintained for several months the evident fiction that taxes would not be raised to finance unification; the pledge was abandoned after the December 1990 general elections. In 1994, the chancellor admitted that he had erred about the timing of his forecast. His new and decidedly more cautious slogan was, 'The new *Länder* are on the way to becoming flourishing landscapes.'[13]

II

The entry of the D-Mark into East Germany in July 1990 heralded reward and retribution, for both East and West. The transposition of East Germans' incomes and savings from East Marks into D-Marks at an overvalued exchange rate, followed by additional increases in wages and social security benefits, fulfilled East Germans' dreams of access to hard currency income. But the currency switch-over also represented an act of colossal economic disablement. It gave 16 million East Germans the opportunity to satisfy their pent-up yearning for western consumer goods, but simultaneously stripped them of the means to earn the future incomes necessary to pay the bill. While East Germans' purchasing power soared, their productive capacity plummeted. To cover the difference between their US-style incomes and Mexican levels of productivity, the Bonn government signed a blank cheque. The huge imbalance between East Germany's aspirations and resources was met by deficit finance on a grand scale. Transfers of public sector funds from West to East Germany approached DM600 billion in the first four years of unity.

An important part of the DM150 billion annual transfers from West to East Germany was spent on improving infrastructure, including measures to clean up the extensive environmental damage left by East Germany's peculiar brand of heedless, inefficient and energy-intensive manufacturing. At the same time, considerable sums were spent on industrial investment. The Bonn government's Treuhand privatisation agency – while running up large debts in the process – succeeded in selling off to western companies a large proportion of East Germany's state-owned industrial enterprises. The Treuhand agency was due to be wound up during 1994, after privatising 13,000 East German companies and, on its own reckoning, securing 1.5 million jobs.[14]

In other fields, too, West German financial help for East Germany was impressive. DM20 billion was spent on improving the run-down East German railways between 1991 and 1993. Road-building benefited to the tune of DM8.8 billion during this period, with a further DM4.2 billion planned for 1994. Under a masssive modernisation programme for telecommunications that planned to spend DM60 billion by 1997, an additional 2.2 million telephone connections were laid between 1991 and 1993, bringing the number of telephones in East Germany up to more than 4 million by 1994.[15]

But for all the impressive effort to renew the decaying East German infrastructure, three-quarters of the cash crossing eastwards was spent on supporting incomes and consumption rather than on capital investment.[16]

By 1993-94, industrial production in East Germany was still more than 50 per cent below pre-unity levels. Productivity, expressed in terms of gross domestic product (output) per worker, was still about 40 per cent of that in West Germany – only slightly higher than the one-third ratio in 1989.[17] By 1993–94, economic recovery in East Germany was at last under way. Considering that West Germany had transferred to the East each year a sum equivalent to double the gross domestic product of Ireland, the economic brightening was not before time.

Transfers to East Germany were partly financed by higher taxes on West German citizens, but they also represented the proceeds of heavy borrowing at home and abroad. During the 1980s, Chancellor Kohl's centre–right government had improved the underlying position of state finances through judicious tax cuts and firm control of spending. As the Germany economy underwent a post-unity metamorphosis, one of the most spectacular victims of German unity was Bonn's previous reputation for fiscal probity and policy-making prudence. Labouring under crises of recession and restructuring in both East and West, by 1993-94 Germany was living well beyond its means. The public sector borrowing requirement, which had been 1 per cent of the West German gross domestic product in 1989, rose to around 5 per cent of GDP in 1994.[18] More than double the level of the US deficit, German borrowing was in line with the average of other European countries – a long way from the levels of 3 per cent of GDP laid down in the Maastricht treaty as the targets for the path towards European monetary union.[19]

The rise in Germany's public sector indebtedness was even more striking. During the first five years of unification, Germany's debts rose by more than West Germany's had done during its previous forty years of existence as a divided country. Towards the end of 1994, overall public sector debt approached DM2 trillion (more than 60 per cent of united Germany's GDP), compared with DM1 billion in West Germany in 1989 (46 per cent of GDP).

In 1989, West Germany ran a surplus on the current account of the balance of payments of 5 per cent of economic output measured by gross domestic product. By 1994, this had switched, for united Germany, to a deficit of 1 per cent of GDP. The annual rate of consumer price inflation rose to 4.2 per cent in 1993 – the highest for a decade – from 2.8 per cent in 1989. Although by 1994 the inflation rate was falling again towards 2 per cent, the improvement in the price climate had been bought at a high price. German unemployment was just under 4 million in 1994, compared with 2 million in West Germany in 1989. Counting the large numbers on short-time working and in government-run job-creation and training schemes (particularly in East Germany), the true number out of work in united Germany in 1993 was estimated at 5.8 million.[20]

Kohl's overconfidence was excessive and mistaken. Partly, it was born of the chancellor's insufficient understanding of economics. Additionally, he showed understandable desire to communicate optimism to the electorate in a manner that would both advance recovery and win elections. Respected figures from the Social Democratic Party also erred in their forecasts of recovery east of the Elbe. Ex-Chancellor Helmut Schmidt, in general a highly sceptical observer of the German economic scene, was wrong when he predicted in 1990 that by 1992 East German unemployment would be starting to fall as economic recovery picked up steam.[21]

Still more telling was the misjudgement of another authoritative politician, Karl Schiller, the legendary former Social Democrat economics minister, past his eightieth birthday but still one of Germany's best respected economic thinkers. In 1990, Schiller foresaw a second 'economic miracle' in East Germany, and declared he was 'astonished' by estimates that unification would cost between DM80 billion and DM100 billion a year. 'These are unsolid calculations.' The West's budgetary help would be limited, he said, to 'start-up financing' (*Anschubfinanzierung*).[22] In later years, however, Schiller voiced increasing criticism of the government's handling of the economic aspects of unification. By 1993-94, he conceded that the notion that only 'start-up financing' was needed had been 'an error'.[23]

Within Kohl's Christian Democratic Union, the only person to challenge the chancellor's misplaced optimism about economic prospects in East Germany was Kurt Biedenkopf, a former CDU general secretary, who in 1990 became prime minister of the East German state of Saxony. Biedenkopf consistently and accurately warned Kohl against underestimating the financial costs of unification. In 1991, he estimated that additional sums of DM90 billion to DM190 billion per year would be needed to finance recovery in the East up to 1995. Although this would be an 'explosive issue' for the next five years, he hoped that West Germans' frustrations would be declining by 1994.[24] In fact, by 1994 frustration over the aftermath of unity had become a permanent feature of life on both sides of the Elbe.

III

Kohl's view was that the introduction of the D-Mark into East Germany would generate the same economic stimulus as the currency reform in June 1948, when the Allies substituted the D-Mark for the Reichsmark in the western zones of occupied Germany. As an eighteen-year-old, the chancellor had lived through the experience of the 1948 reform in his native Rhineland-Palatinate. In later years, he had savoured accounts of what had happened, as described, for instance, in an oft-cited book published in 1953: 'The black market disappeared in the most sudden fashion. The shop windows were bursting full with goods, smoke issued from factory chimneys, and the streets teemed with lorries. Everywhere, the deadly hush of ruins was replaced by the hustle and bustle of building sites.'[25] In 1990, Kohl believed the process would simply be repeated.

Kohl branded critics of the East Mark conversion as lacking vision, courage or intelligence, more often than not all three: 'If Erhard had thought like that, then today we would still be buying shoes with rationing coupons.'[26] Kohl did not recognise that the episodes of June 1948 and July 1990 were not comparable. In 1948, the whole of Europe was still recovering from war. East Germany in 1990-91 was in a far more disadvantaged position compared with the rest of the continent than was West Germany in 1948-49.

In 1948, the advent of the D-Mark revitalised West Germany's industry; in 1990, exposure of East Germany's moribund industrial capacity to the cold wind of western competition led to most of it being eliminated. In 1948, West Germany's industrial production rose 50 per cent in the first six months after the introduction of the

D-Mark.[27] In 1990, in the first six months of monetary union, East Germany's industrial production fell 50 per cent. Economist Holger Schmieding described the effect on East Germany as 'probably the gravest economic crisis ever to befall an advanced industrial economy in peacetime.'[28] For two years – until the upturn started in 1993–94 – East German production remained at the low level of the second half of 1990.

Ex-Chancellor Schmidt identified the central reason why the introduction of the D-Mark was fundamentally different from the 1948 reform.[29] 'At the end of the war, all entrepreneurs and employees, all producers and all consumers in the old Federal Republic were exposed to the same conditions, both material and spiritual. Everyone, or nearly everyone, had gone hungry, nearly everyone started from nothing . . . For the East German companies, the circumstances after the 1990 monetary treaty were completely different. Overnight they had to come to grips with an unaccustomed environment, with which their western competitors had decades of experience.'[30]

The decision to bring the D-Mark to East Germany did not reflect a well thought-out strategy. Rather, it was the result of near-panic in Bonn in early 1990 over the growing chaos in East Germany. Kohl's earlier plans, in the immediate aftermath of the fall of the Berlin Wall, forcsaw a much more leisurely pace of 'growing together' between East and West Germany. His ten-point plan for German unification unveiled at the end of November 1989 laid down a cautious plan for 'confederal structures' between East and West, rather than the dash for unity that ensued.[31]

In the first few months of 1990, however, as 2,000 East Germans a day crossed the Elbe to seek new lives in West Germany, one factor above all else motivated the Bonn governnment: fear. Kohl knew he had to issue a signal of hope to the East German population to encourage them to stay in the East. The conclusion drawn in Bonn was that, if East Germany's population was not to be emptied to the West, wages had to be raised to nearer western levels, and the battered, inconvertible East Mark had to be replaced by the D-Mark.

There was, in fact, evidence that lack of jobs caused by excessive East German wages, rather than lack of income, would be the main stimulus for migration.[32] The entry of the D-Mark, accompanied by the full panoply of West Germany's economic system, could not be a panacea for the East's afflictions. That would require a self-sustaining economic recovery – which was still years away. Although at a lower level, flows of East Germans to the West continued long after DM27.5 billion worth of new currency – 460 tonnes of notes and 600 tonnes of coins – was eventually transported into East Germany at the end of June.

The atmosphere in Bonn in early 1990, however, was not conducive to rational policy discussion. German economic policy was being made not in the parlours of government, but on the streets of Berlin, Leipzig and Dresden. As East Germany came in from the cold, its inhabitants were no longer afraid of the state security service. Instead, they feared being left alone without the D-Mark. In countless street demonstrations, they sounded a warning incantation to the Bonn government. Their slogan had the mesmeric quality of a couplet from a Grimm fairy tale: *'Kommt die D-Mark, bleiben wir. Kommt sie nicht, geh'n wir zu ihr.'* ('If the D-Mark comes, we stay here. If it doesn't come, we'll go to the D-Mark.')

It was a potent threat, and one that had to be countered with an equally powerful financial inducement for the East Germans to stay firmly where they were. In March 1990, Kohl admitted: 'If we don't carry out economic and monetary union, then we face the risk that in the summer we will have 500,000 people coming here from the GDR.'[33] Wolfgang Röller, the chief executive of Germany's second largest bank, Dresdner Bank – which adopted a wholly unrealistic optimism about growth prospects for the East German economy – warned that a 'political time bomb' was ticking in the East;[34] the D-Mark was the only means of defusing it. A day after Unity Day in 1990, Kohl adopted still more extreme language in defending the step to extend the D-Mark to the East. 'If we had not introduced economic and monetary union on 1 July, we would have had by now roughly one million emigrés from the GDR, which would have caused catastrophic social upheavals in the Federal Republic and in the GDR.'[35]

The fundamental decision to press ahead with German monetary union was made hurriedly, amid much confusion. During a hectic period in January and February 1990, the Bonn government gave contradictory signals on its views and intentions. Its central dilemma was a familiar one, experienced repeatedly in different forms during the past thirty years of grappling with *Deutschlandpolitik*: would financial stabilisation of East Germany bring unification closer, or would it simply shore up support for the bankrupt East Berlin regime?

The original suggestion of monetary union between the Federal Republic and the GDR was made in mid-January 1990 by the Social Democratic Party.[36] Mainly for reasons of party politics, it was promptly rejected by the Bonn government, on the grounds that it would needlessly bolster the East German regime. On 19 January 1990, Waigel ruled out an 'artificially inspired' monetary union as 'a dangerous and completely wrong signal.'[37] On 25 January, he repeated it was 'too early' for any such step, which would not only be 'ineffective' but would also 'endanger monetary stability.'[38] A special report from the government's council of independent economic advisers – the so-called 'wise men' – pointed out that the East Mark was a currency 'of only very limited convertibility' and recommended against associating the Bundesbank with any attempt to stabilise it.[39] Taking their cue from the 'wise men' as well as from Waigel, Karl Otto Pöhl, the Bundesbank president, rebuffed the idea of monetary union as 'fantastic';[40] his deputy, Helmut Schlesinger, called it 'very unrealistic.'[41]

In early February, Kohl became convinced that further East German migration would disrupt both East and West. Impulsively, he made up his mind. To prevent the East Germans coming westwards, the D-Mark would, indeed, go to the East Germans. After he met Hans Modrow, the East German prime minister, on the weekend of 3–4 February, and then East German conservative opposition leaders on the evening of 5 February, Kohl concluded that an offer of monetary union was essential; and it had to be incontrovertibly tied to the prospect of full political union. At a meeting in the Bonn chancellor's office at 10 a.m. on 6 February, in which Horst Teltschik, his foreign affairs specialist, and other staff advisers on East Germany took part, Kohl decided to propose early negotiations on transferring the D-Mark across the Elbe.[42]

The momentous decision was announced that afternoon in Bonn, before the government had time to inform

Bundesbank president Pöhl, who had travelled to East Berlin on 6 February for talks with the East German central bank. Pöhl had met Finance Minister Waigel in Bonn the previous evening to analyse the impact of developments in East Germany. Both men shared a taste for irreverent humour, but otherwise there was little in their personalities and still less in their politics to unite the Social Democrat Pöhl and the conservative South German finance minister. Pöhl, whose habitually tanned features hide a thin skin, had never completely forgiven Waigel for having previously opposed his nomination to the Bundesbank job.[43]

Their two hours of talks in Waigel's cramped Rhineside offices were convivial enough, but – since the monetary union decision was not taken until the following morning – the two men had little of substance to say to each other. Pöhl, who had just arrived back in Germany from a visit to the US, did not realise that the flood of East German arrivals had placed Bonn in a state of alarm. A few days earlier, Waigel – aware of Kohl's increasingly dire assessment of the consequences of East German migration – had shifted his ground on the desirability of monetary union. On 2 February, the Finance Ministry issued a statement saying the introduction of the D-Mark could be 'necessary . . . to offer the people of the GDR a convincing perspective for the future.'[44] However, Waigel, like Pöhl, did not realise the imminence of the monetary union announcement.

In his exchange of views with Pöhl on 5 February, Waigel hinted that West Germany might have to assume monetary responsibility for East Germany. But he did so in a highly oblique fashion, casually citing a German-dubbed catch-phrase from the US detective serial *Mission Impossible*, a favourite programme on German

TV. Indicating that the East German authorities could soon ask the West Germans to intervene in the manner of a police investigation squad, Waigel attempted to prepare Pöhl for the extension of the Bundesbank's jurisdiction into East Germany with the following words: '*Kobra – übernehmen Sie!*' ('Cobra, take over control').[45] The Bundesbank president ascribed no great importance to the finance minister's 'Cobra' reference. Waigel, after all, was well known for his wisecracks.

The meeting between Pöhl and Waigel marked a seminal moment in the reunification saga. Using the D-Mark as the prime instrument of unification was an act of monumental significance for Germany and its European partners. Not only did it pave the way for East German economic collapse; it was also to become an important factor behind the disruption of the European Monetary System, as Britain and France discovered in 1992–93. Yet the step was taken without proper consultation, not only with Germany's partners, but also within the highest echelons of the German economic establishment. The misunderstanding between Waigel and Pöhl illustrated the haste and opacity of the decision-making process. Seldom in the field of economic history had a step of such consequence been prepared with so little forethought.

Once the announcement was made, there was no turning back. East Germans stepped up street demonstrations demanding that savings in East Marks be exchanged into D-Marks on a 1 for 1 basis. 'One for one, or we will never be one,' was their cry. Asked for its advice, the Bundesbank at the end of March suggested a 1 for 2 conversion rate between D-Marks and East Marks. The central bank was, however, overruled after protests from East Germans complaining that anything other than 1 to 1 would unfairly reduce their savings and leave them with wages of only one quarter of western levels. Agreement on a more generous conversion rate, based on 1 for 1 for wages and smaller savings deposits, with a 1 for 2 rate for larger accounts, was announced on 23 April.[46] Although current payments such as wages were to be converted at 1 for 1, the average exchange rate used for translating savings accounts was 1 to 1.8 – closer in line to the original Bundesbank suggestion.

East Germany's first and last democratically elected prime minister, Lothar de Maizière, who played a significant part in organising the campaign for the 1 for 1 conversion, conceded afterwards that the generous exchange rate was 'a gift', since the East Mark was 'backed by nothing'.[47] The official view of the two German states, however, was that the terms were correct. The treaty on monetary union signed in May 1990 between the Federal Republic and the GDR even stated that the overall exchange rate could be made still more favourable to easterners if subsequent investigation showed that West Germany had underestimated the strength of East Germany's finances.[48]

IV

In 1990, there was no shortage of well-founded predictions that the terms for the conversion from East Marks into D-Marks would be highly expensive. A year later, Otto Schlecht, the most senior civil servant in the Economics Ministry at the time of unification, admitted why such warnings were largely disregarded. 'We deceived ourselves about the size and depth of the restructuring crisis. We gave prominence to the positive elements [about East German economic prospects] and forced the negative ones into the background. This was because we wanted people to take heart – and because there was an election campaign.'[49] And in 1993, from his subsequent vantage point as president of the free-market Ludwig-Erhard Foundation, Schlecht issued his own sombre predictions about the risk of a 'Mezzogiorno syndrome' in which East Germany, like southern Italy, would be permanently subsidised by fiscal transfers from the richer part of the country.[50]

Examining East Germany's predicament in 1993, Horst Teltschik, Kohl's former foreign affairs adviser, who subsequently became a member of the management board of the BMW car company, said West Germany had under-estimated the East Germans' psychological difficulties in reacting to the shock of unification. Their 'shattered consciousness' and 'spiritual separation' had emerged as the main handicaps to speedy economic revival. 'We saw the consequences of fifty years of history.'[51] Teltschik recalled the general belief in 1990 that two-thirds of East German enterprises might survive – some after intensive restructuring – while one-third would go bankrupt.[52] This appeared a rigorous enough analysis in 1990, but, according to Teltschik's later thinking, it was based on 'pure illusion' about the East German economy. In fact, only one-third survived, while two-thirds disappeared.

In February 1990, only a few failed to believe in illusions. Bundesbank president Pöhl was the only senior policy-maker to state publicly his qualms, forecasting that entry of the D-Mark at a level that substantially overvalued the East Mark would cause the closure of much of East German industry. This would make necessary 'enormous transfer payments' from the West to ward off the danger of 'social upheaval.'[53] Other less well-known Bundesbank officials also spoke out. In May 1990, a week before the monetary union treaty was signed, Helmut Hesse, president of the Land central bank of Lower Saxony, and a member of the Bundesbank's policy-making council, said: 'We must now fear serious strains. In particular, unemployment, a rise in West German transfer payments to the German Democratic Republic and higher public sector debt can all be expected.'[54]

One of Germany's leading economic research institutes, the Berlin-based Deutsches Institut für Wirtschaftsforschung, forecast in February 1990 that the introduction of the D-Mark, combined with rising East German wages towards West German levels, would result in 'a large part of East German industry [being] no longer competitive', causing large-scale plant closures and redundancies.[55] Professor Hans Karl Schneider, the chairman of the government's council of economic advisers, stated that tax rises would be necessary to defray the costs of the D-Mark conversion.[56] The government ignored the message for nearly a year.

West Germany's five leading economic research institutes warned in April 1990 that the 'ostensible gift' of a favourable East Mark exchange rate would be 'purchased with many job losses.'[57] Oskar Lafontaine, the Saarland prime minister, fighting an uphill battle as the Social Democrats' candidate for the chancellorship in the December 1990 general elections, tried vainly to make political capital out of the costs of unification. When he predicted in summer 1990 that unity would cost DM100 billion a year, he was mocked by the government. In fact, Lafontaine's figure turned out to be an underestimate.[58]

A master of the art of verbal obfuscation, Waigel

brushed aside the sceptics in March 1990 with well-practised aplomb:

> In the last few weeks I have received almost daily analyses and reports warning about a rapid monetary union and too quick an integration of the two German economies. Certainly, if there was sufficient time, it would be more convincing, from an economic point of view, to carry out economic and monetary union at the end of a process of aligning the [two] economic areas, a period which would have been used to adapt the GDR economic system and overcome its productivity lag. However, the drama of developments in the GDR, and the understandable impatience of the people there, call for quick solutions . . .
>
> Much has recently been written about the size of the necessary capital transfers to East Germany, and about the time required for economic catch-up. But many who are now carrying out their calculations of billions [of marks] know little about the way our social market economy works. Certainly, East Germany will depend heavily on capital imports. But this capital, which must above all be private capital, will flow by itself, as soon as investment in the GDR becomes worthwhile . . .
>
> A second German economic miracle is thoroughly possible. In the light of these perspectives, all the calculations about the burdens of unification will soon be refuted.[59]

In early 1990, some foreign economists predicted that unification could cost an annual DM100 billion.[60] But at the time that monetary union was under debate in Bonn no mainstream German economist put forward an estimate of more than DM50 billion a year for public sector financing of the East – only one third of the

figure that later materialised.[61] Most were still more
sanguine. Dresdner Bank was particularly optimistic,
estimating western Germany would face a net public
sector burden of only around DM20 billion a year.
'Inflationary expectations of 5 per cent and demands
on the capital markets of DM100 billion a year are
way beyond probability.'[62] Wolfgang Röller, its chief
executive, launched an outspoken attack on critics of
monetary union, saying that every newspaper article
or TV film raising 'fears' about the future could increase
unemployment in East Germany.[63] Dresdner's miscalculation puts a wry perspective on complaints in 1993 –
when the mood had turned much more sombre – by
Röller's successor. Jürgen Sarrazin, who took over in
1992, criticised other members of the European Community for not doing enough to help ease Germany's
unification burdens.[64]

Another overconfident projection came from the
Cologne-based Institut der deutschen Wirtschaft, which
forecast East German productivity could double during
the forthcoming decade, enabling East Germany to catch
up with West German output levels by 2000.[65] In spring
1991, dissent on the subject emerged in the auspicious
surroundings of an informal and unpublicised meeting
in Stockholm of the chairmen of some of the world's
biggest banks. Top West German bankers launched an
unusual reprimand of Sir David Scholey, the chairman
of Britain's merchant bank S.G. Warburg, for suggesting
that unification could overstretch Germany's financial
resources.[66]

In 1990, the doubters emphasising the economic difficulties of German monetary union faced an
overwhelming disadvantage. Apart from suggesting
that reunification should be slowed down – an option

that the people of East Germany manifestly did not want – they could formulate no plausible alternative to pressing ahead with the introduction of the D-Mark as soon as possible. One option would have been to associate the entry of the D-Mark with a lengthy transition period in which government action would have been required to hold down wages and restrict consumption in East Germany. This could have been made the essential condition for directing fiscal resources eastwards to rebuild the economy. Such a measure would have made explicit the East Germans' need to live until the end of the 1990s with markedly lower incomes than those in the West. A programme of this kind would have clearly exposed Germany's fragmentation into a two-tier society split between East and West. But, combined with a rigorous message to West Germans that sacrifices were needed to make a success of unity, it would have been a more realistic way of solving Germany's unity crisis than Kohl's unsound promise of quick rewards.

V

In July 1990, when the currency conversion took effect, the survival of many East German industrial enterprises was in doubt. Their fate was sealed when, in the ensuing twelve months, East German wages started to rise rapidly towards those in the West. Starting at 34 per cent of those in the West in the second half of 1990, the level rose to 47 per cent in 1991, 62 per cent in 1992 and 70 per cent in 1993.[67] Relying on political promises of subsidies to bail out the Treuhand-owned companies, East German trade unions were keen to demonstrate muscle-power to their members. The shift towards wage alignment was also encouraged by western trade unions promoting nationwide 'social solidarity' as a means of maintaining high wages in the West.[68] Moreover, the campaign for equal wages was also driven, at least in part, by West German companies with representatives on East German enterprises' supervisory boards. They frequently had keen commercial interest in agreeing to uneconomic wage rises, since this provided an effective way of hastening the closure of potential competition.[69]

The overvalued level chosen for the East Mark in 1990 would have been less of a problem had the East German cost squeeze on enterprises been reduced through such means as targeted wage subsidies or 'employment bonuses'. These would have required the government to pay East German companies a specific proportion of their wage costs – perhaps up to 75 per cent – to maintain profitability and employment.[70] Such subsidies would have been conditional on agreement on East German wage restraint. They would have been partly self-financing, through the effect of reducing state spending on unemployment benefits and raising tax and social security contributions. Innovative proposals for increasing the economic viability of East German companies were sporadically put forward in 1990-91. There is, however, no evidence that the Bonn government ever took them seriously.[71]

As savings and incomes were switched into D-Marks and wages and social security benefits rose towards western levels, the East Germans forsook the shabby wares of communist autarky in favour of long sought-after products from the West. The effect on the East German economy was amplified by developments in eastern Europe. The Bonn government had been hoping to maintain East Germany's strong trade links with the Soviet Union and central and eastern Europe. However, these were badly hit in 1990-91 by the collapse of the Comecon trading system that linked the Soviet Union and the other former East bloc countries. The combination of increased competition from western industry and the sudden disintegration of previously stable export markets led to a fall of 15 per cent in East Germany's gross domestic product in 1990. The next year, when Bonn had been anticipating an upturn, turned out even worse: GDP fell 31 per cent.[72]

Overall East German unemployment (counting people in short-time working and job-training schemes) rose to 30 per cent of the labour force, compared with the pre-1990 position where the number out of work had been (officially) close to zero. In 1991, 1992 and 1993, overall East German demand was respectively 195 per cent, 185 per cent and 174 per cent of GDP. This was a dramatic illustration of the gulf between East German incomes and productivity that had to be filled by transfers of funds from West Germany.[73] The crumbling of East Germany's economic foundations magnified overall German budgetary strains. Additionally, the brutality of the adjustment to capitalism exacerbated East German disgruntlement about the hardships of unification.

Between 1989 and 1992 the East German labour force contracted from 10 million people to 6 million, of whom 1.4 million became unemployed, and 1 million were on short-time working or in job creation schemes.[74] The 4 million who left the labour force retired, emigrated, died, or simply stayed at home. Although the East German economy grew by an annual average of 8.5 per cent between 1992 and 1994, it was evident that the ground lost in the first twelve months after unification would take years to make up. On realistic assumptions,

2010 was the earliest possible date by which East and West Germany might achieve a measure of economic convergence.

In the first year after unity, East Germany's losses were West Germany's gains. The initial effects of unification reinforced the impression of West German supremacy – another powerful factor impeding prospects for convergence. The terms of the D-Mark–East Mark conversion, along with heavy Bonn government expenditure on social security and infrastructure in the East, generated enormous eastern spending power. Channelled back westwards across the Elbe in the form of higher demand for western goods, this produced GDP growth of 5.7 per cent in West Germany in 1990, the highest rate of expansion since 1969. West Germany's flurry of above-average growth lasted until 1992: an exceptional climax to a decade-long period of economic buoyancy that had started, modestly at first, after the 1981-82 recession.

This phase of economic overheating buttressed the belief of at least some West Germans that unification could be accomplished without significant cost. But as the budget deficit expanded, it became clear that a high price was being paid for extra economic growth. As one German economist remarked with prescience in early 1991: 'This has been the biggest-ever Keynesian boom in Germany. We will have to pay the bill in three or four years' time with higher taxes.'[75]

VI

In the twelfth floor directorate offices of the Bundesbank, there were distinct differences of emphasis over

German unification – an apt reflection of divergences across German society as a whole. The Bundesbank had supported the more realistic 1 for 2 rate for the D-Mark–East Mark conversion. But most senior officials at the central bank backed Kohl's unification strategy, even if they knew it involved considerable risks. In their public statements, these officials generally balanced carefully-chosen words of scepticism over the terms of German monetary union with a message of support for unity. In later years, this provided them with ample evidence to show that, in whatever question had been under discussion, their judgement had invariably been correct.

Pöhl, the central bank's president up to 1991, was the most agnostic about unification, both before and after it happened. He made no secret that his preference would have been for the two Germanys to cooperate with each other as separate states.[76] In Brussels in March 1991, Pöhl told a committee of the European parliament that the monetary union conversion terms had produced a 'disaster' in East Germany. The off-the-cuff remarks provoked dismay and hostility in Bonn – an important reason for Pöhl's resignation two months later. As a Social Democrat, and a man easily irritated by Kohl's verbosity, Pöhl had never been on close terms with the chancellor. Relations subsequently grew bitter. In 1993, more than two years after Pöhl's departure, Kohl still harboured resentment about the former Bundesbank president's criticism of his unification policies.[77] For his part, Pöhl – who subsequently became the part-time chief executive of the Cologne-based Oppenheim private bank – remained defiant: 'The chancellor did not like the remark [in Brussels]. But it was not wrong.'[78]

Schlesinger, the Bundesbank's vice-president under

Pöhl for eleven and a half years, who succeeded him for two years from 1991, had been initially highly doubtful about taking the D-Mark into East Germany. But, in contrast to Pöhl, he gave unremitting support to reunification, and left no doubt about his loyalty to the government. A conservative economist who had joined the Bank deutscher Länder, the Bundesbank's predecessor, in 1952, Schlesinger's political affiliations were to the Bavarian Christian Social Union (although he was not a member), giving him a natural affinity with the chancellor. Schlesinger's instinctive belief, from 1990 onwards, was that the exacting nature of German unification would preclude a rapid move to European economic and monetary union. To avoid upsetting delicate negotiations with Germany's European partners, Schlesinger kept his doubts about Emu out of the limelight, yet his prudence turned out to be fully justified. But even the austere Schlesinger was over-optimistic in his assessment of East German economic prospects. In 1991, he forecast, in a treatise published with two colleagues, that Germany's public sector debt by the end of 1994 would be around DM1.6 trillion. The assumptions on which the calculation were based appeared realistic. However, it turned out to be one of Schlesinger's least accurate predictions. He underestimated the total by more than DM400 billion.[79]

Of the members of the Bundesbank's dominant triumverate in the early 1990s, Hans Tietmeyer was by far the most outspoken proponent of unification. He joined the central bank in 1990 as directorate member for international affairs after, having served as state secretary in the Bonn Finance Ministry since 1982. After taking over Schlesinger's job as vice-president upon Pöhl's resignation in 1991, Tietmeyer moved to the helm of the Bundesbank in October 1993 when Schlesinger retired. Tietmeyer, a Christian Democrat party member, is one of Kohl's closest economic policy confidants. He is also one of the few German officials with the self-esteem to stand up to the chancellor in private conversation.

In April 1990, Tietmeyer was seconded from the Bundesbank to become Kohl's personal economic adviser on unification. As the head of the West German delegation negotiating the treaty on German monetary union implemented in July 1990, Tietmeyer was thus the main Bundesbank official to share personal responsibility for the terms of the 1990 monetary conversion. Even though he had helped fashion it, Tietmeyer afterwards took a critical view of the outcome, commenting in 1991 that the Bundesbank's 1 for 2 proposal for the D-Mark–East Mark rate 'would have been more favourable both for the competitiveness of East German industry and for the necessity of maintaining wage differentials [between the two parts of Germany]. Unfortunately, it was not possible to put the proposal into effect.' The result, he added, was much lower East German competitiveness after monetary union, and higher unemployment.[80]

In a rare admission in 1991, Tietmeyer conceded that, because of pressure of time, the treaty contained other important flaws.[81] In particular, he acknowledged the error of permitting former owners of property in East Germany to reclaim their assets through arduous legal action, rather than asking them to forgo their assets in return for state compensation. This decision was made to shield the government from the need to make large payments for financial redress. But the time taken to identify ownership of land and assets and disentangle competing claims subsequently posed considerable hurdles to economic reconstruction.

Like many other members of the West German economic establishment, Tietmeyer in 1990 took an overfavourable view of East Germany's productivity, which he said might be around half the West German level[82] – 50 per cent higher than the figure turned out to be. In 1994, Tietmeyer adopted a remarkably fatalistic tone on the errors committed in 1990, which, he implied, resulted in part from foreigners' overestimation of East Germany's industrial capacity. 'The surprise in the west of Germany about the exceedingly poor condition of the East German economy was very great, partly because, for a long period, international [economic] institutions had termed the then German Democratic Republic as the tenth strongest industrial state [in the world].'[83]

As this remark implied, in 1993–94 Germany's top policy-makers tended to ascribe the tortuous aftermath of unity to a mixture of fate, ill-fortune and inaccurate East German statistics, obscuring the role played by their own poor judgement. The 1990–91 collapse of Comecon markets for East German goods was, for instance, frequently cited as an unforeseeable setback. In October 1993, Kohl dismissed the elimination of East Germany's traditional markets in the East as 'bad luck'.[84] The speed of decline of East German exports to central and eastern Europe, magnified by the sharp drop in output across the area as the former members of the Soviet bloc adjusted to life after communism, was indeed far greater than expected. But the switch in these states' foreign trade was not a surprise.[85] The former East bloc countries no longer had recourse to the soft payment terms of the old Comecon system, since they were required from 1991 onwards to pay for their imports from East Germany in

D-Marks. It was therefore logical that these countries – provided they had available reserves of foreign exchange – should shift their purchases away from East Germany towards the far higher quality goods available in the West.[86] After all, the prime tenet of the new economic system in which central and eastern Europe found itself was that purchasers had freedom of choice.

VII

Bonn's failure to put unity financing on a sound footing was bound to have important consequences for monetary policy. To counter inflationary pressures and the threat of financial instability, the Bundesbank had little choice but to turn to the blunt instrument of interest rate increases. Shortly after his resignation as Bundesbank president in 1991, Pöhl predicted that the central bank was about to engineer the first German recession for more than a decade.[87] In 1992-93, the forecast turned out to be correct.

At a time when Germany was raising massive volumes of capital from international banks and investment institutions, maintaining credibility in the value of the German currency was vitally important. Growing fiscal deficits and the rise in Germany's inflation rate to more than 4 per cent signalled extreme disequilibrium in the German economy, sparking three increases in 1991 in the Bundesbank's main interest rate – the discount rate – after more than a year in which it had been left unchanged.

In the circumstances, the Bundesbank's determination to adhere to tough anti-inflationary policies was undoubtedly the right decision for Germany, even though it had detrimental repercussions for the rest of Europe. In the last full year of Pöhl's stewardship, 1990, the Bundesbank made a serious error in failing to tighten the interest rate screw, in spite of signs of West Germany's severe economic overheating. Prompt monetary tightening in 1990 would have had a salutary effect in Germany and the rest of Europe, since it would have obviated the need to make abrupt interest rate increases later on.[88]

In November 1991, the clouds of recession started to gather. Johann Eekhoff, state secretary in the Economics Ministry, who had taken over from Otto Schlecht in 1991 as the ministry's top civil servant, made an impassioned plea for a breakthrough on the wage bargaining front to restore economic equilibrium. Pointing out that only half East Germany's income was being met by production, he called on West Germans to 'give up' entitlements to increases in wages, profits and public spending to finance the necessary transfers of resources to the East. The decisive question was, he said:

> Is our society ready to limit wages and incomes to no more than anticipated increases in productivity? Or – in view of the contradictory nature of all these claims on our resources – do we stagger resignedly into the expensive lesson of a serious recession? The result would be much larger reductions in income for everyone in East and West.[89]

Eekhoff's warning went unheeded. The recession arrived, as if pre-ordained.

As the economic news grew more difficult, so did the political task of achieving a consensus between Kohl's Christian Democrats and the opposition Social Democrats on cutting the budget deficit. In 1993, Otmar

Issing, the Bundesbank board member responsible for economics, outlined the fiscal strains with poignant clarity: 'The longer the process lasts, the clearer it becomes that the state faces a cumulation of old and new tasks and obligations that hopelessly exceeds its capacity to meet them.'[90]

The Christian Democrats' grip over economic policy-making was weakened by a succession of setbacks for Kohl's party in *Land* (state) elections around the country. These gave the Social Democrats a majority in the Bundesrat, the upper house of parliament, which comprises the representatives of the *Länder* and has veto power over important aspects of economic decision-making, including tax policy. Complicating the question further, many of the increases in Germany's fiscal deficits in the early 1990s were instigated by the *Länder* and municipalities, over whose borrowing the central government had no control.

Germany's method of spreading tax receipts according to the wealth of different parts of the country (the so-called *Länderfinanzausgleich* system) had always been one of the strengths of the country's economic and political structure. In relatively homogeneous pre-unity West Germany, it functioned well. However, attempts after 1990 to work out a more equitable means of distributing fiscal resources among the highly disparate *Länder* of East and West Germany were bedevilled by the western states' desire to limit reductions in their income. As soon as Germany encompassed not eleven but sixteen states separated by much larger divergences in income and prosperity, the system became a great deal less easy to operate. Germany's decentralised federal structure played a highly successful role in promoting recovery after 1949, but it hindered the search for better economic balance in the more difficult circumstances of the post-unity era.

VIII

By 1993, four years after the fall of the Wall, the Bonn government had hoped that East Germany would be well on the way to recovery. However, the Organisation for Economic Cooperation and Development (OECD), in its annual report that year on the German economy, forecast that united Germany was still only at the start of a long journey:

> While the transfer of all western social, legal and administrative institutions to the eastern *Länder* has occurred smoothly, and privatisation of a large part of the previously state-owned capital stock has been achieved rapidly, a costly and lengthy task of rebuilding still lies ahead.[91]

Reflecting the destruction of industrial capacity in 1990-91, East Germany will need considerably longer than earlier anticipated even to approach the average levels of economic output and productivity of the West. In 1990, the OECD had predicted that East Germany would need at least fifteen years to eliminate its economic lag, assuming annual eastern growth rates of 7.5 per cent – similar to actual growth in West Germany during the 1950s.[92] By 1993, it became clear that, assuming annual growth rates of 2 per cent in the West and 7 per cent in the East, East Germany would require until the year 2012 to improve output per head even to 80 per cent of the West German level.[93] If the East German growth rate is less than this – or the West German rate is higher

– then the time needed will be even longer. Whatever happens, another generation will have to pass before economic and social unification is complete.

A fundamental reason for post-unity disequilibrium has been the refusal of either East or West Germans to make sacrifices in incomes to finance the burdens of unification. Stubbornness will have to make way for flexibility. The need for fiscal transfers from West to East will gradually decline as the gap between East German production and demand narrows. West Germany will none the less have to channel across the Elbe sums of at least DM100 billion a year up to the end of the 1990s. These transfers will be financed by reductions in West German purchasing power. This can take place either involuntarily, through additional taxation, or voluntarily, through agreement on cuts in real (inflation-adjusted) wages, as happened in recession-hit West German industry in 1993-94. East German workers, for their part, will have to defer until the late 1990s plans for wage equality with West Germany. In 1993, East German metalworkers agreed to delay wage 'catch-up', originally planned for 1994, to 1996. A further postponement seems both essential and inevitable.

During the rest of the 1990s, Germany will be walking an economic tightrope. The combination of a big increase in taxation and an even larger addition to government borrowing has greatly limited room for budgetary manoeuvre. East Germany's prospects will depend heavily on West German and foreign companies treating the region as a production base and not simply as a region in which to distribute goods made elsewhere. Competition from products from neighbouring low-wage countries in central and eastern Europe will be an exacting problem. At the heart of East Germany's economic troubles lies a perplexing conundrum. The productivity gap compared with West Germany will remain very high unless there is a considerable increase in private sector investment in plant and machinery in East Germany in coming years. However, as long as this productivity gap persists, East Germany is unlikely to tempt corporate investors from West Germany and abroad in sufficient numbers to bring significant reductions in unemployment. The Bonn government's strategy of providing large-scale tax incentives and subsidies for investment in the East has been flawed, since this has encouraged high-cost and ultimately uneconomic production. Self-supporting economic recovery in East Germany will come only when the cost of production falls sufficiently to make investments there worthwhile.[94]

Transforming East Germany from a region which simply consumes West German incomes into an area of autonomous economic activity will take time. East Germans have already faced an abundance of toil and transition. Their task of adjustment will run for years to come. Until it is complete, the whole of Europe will share the strain.

Storm and Repair

The only capital which Germany still possesses is its capacity for work . . . In the long run, Germany can live only as a capital-intensive, highly industrialised state, but this is a far-off goal.

Marion Gräfin Dönhoff, future publisher of Die Zeit, *1947*[1]

West Germany was a model only during the post-war recovery, when markets were developing faster than institutions. Now, the corporatist structure of organised interest groups is again coming to the fore. What we need is a consensus for more flexibility – but the organisations are not receptive.

Professor Herbert Giersch, president,
Kiel Economic Research Institute, 1987[2]

In two or three years' time, German industry will have recovered brilliantly. The share of manufacturing in gross domestic product will be lower, but we will be fully competitive. Industry will have rationalised away the expensive job places, with lower cost production taking place increasingly in eastern Europe and high technology in Asia. We will preserve the heart of our economic system. But the concept of 'Made in Germany' will be replaced by 'Designed in Germany'.

Ludolf von Wartenberg, general manager,
Federation of German Industry (BDI), 1994[3]

I

Modern Germany's history follows a trail of economic vicissitude. German business cycles are epic bursts of storm and repair, sending out tremors that rock the path of national destiny. During a mere three decades, between 1920 and 1950, under democracy, dictatorship and Allied occupation, Germany weathered a span of dreams and disaster: hyperinflation and slump; rearmament-driven revival; war, destruction and division; and then the beginning of a long upturn. The attributes that nurtured the economic renaissance of the 1950s and 1960s – moderation, hard work, reliability, efficiency – became near-mythological hallmarks of a new and better Germany. The 'economic miracle' – a term the Germans regarded with disfavour, for it suggested that the process was due purely to good fortune[4] – gave the country a fresh start in a renovated Europe. By profiting from and contributing to the stability of the continent, the West Germans created a new identity. With it, they laid the groundwork for another feat of reconstruction that eventually started long after most had abandoned hope of witnessing it: the reforging of nationhood.

East Germany's fall in 1989-90 came amid a sudden

acceleration in the pulse of the international economy. Worldwide deregulation combined with revolutions in technology and communications increased the pace of interchange of goods, people, money and ideas across five continents. Within the European Community, the development between 1987 and 1992 of the barrier-free 'single market' stoked western Europe's creative energies through fresh liberalisation of trade and commerce.

East German leader Erich Honecker had boasted in 1981 that, one day, socialism would 'knock on the door' of West Germany;[5] in November 1989, the East Berlin regime watched in glum impotence as the forces of West German capitalism first knocked on and then beat down East Germany's portals. Everywhere, across a state that had previously been the strongest outpost of the Soviet empire, faded propaganda signs expressing desperate conviction that *'Der Marxismus dauert ewig'* (Marxism lasts forever) were dismantled and cast on the refuse dump of European history. Yet if East Germany's disintegration provided a graphic illustration of the power of global economic integration, so too did the speed with which the after-shocks spread beyond Germany's frontiers.

Capitalism's entry into East Germany – 'a great, virtually unprecedented experiment,' as Karl Schiller called it[6] – was a moment of triumph for the West German economic system. Few predicted that unification would also bring its greatest test. It was a denouement of which Marx might have been grudgingly appreciative. Communism's contradictions felled East Germany and then, in the years afterwards, exerted a disruptive impact on the state that was its successor. The hydraulic fluid of the international market economy washed away the Berlin Wall, and then transmitted the pain of adjustment throughout capitalist Europe.

As German budget deficits mounted in the early 1990s, German public sector borrowers increased overall foreign debt by more than DM250 billion to nearly DM500 billion in the three years between the end of 1990 and the end of 1993.[7] Since this indebtedness largely resulted from foreigners' purchases of German government securities on the bond markets, rather than though the launch of specially organised credits, most Germans were unaware that their country had become a large foreign borrower. Germany continued to boast large net foreign assets.[8] However, the need to maintain large capital inflows and preserve confidence in the D-Mark at a time of great economic uncertainty left the Bundesbank with no choice but to maintain tight monetary policies between 1990 and 1993. This, in turn, was a critical factor behind the high interest rates throughout Europe, which worsened the continent-wide economic downturn in 1992-93, and provided a fresh impediment for the Maastricht plan for a single European currency by the end of the century. Chancellor Kohl's much-repeated adage was that 'German unity and European unity are two sides of the same coin.'[9] When the economics of German unity went awry, both sides of the coin lost their shine.

II

If unification provided an extreme trial for the resources of the West German economy, it had at least been able to devote forty years to building them up. Even though it had lost some of its most dynamic characteristics in the 1970s and 1980s, by the time of reunification Germany was long established as Europe's leading economy.

As West Germany's economic influence spread throughout eastern and western Europe during the post-war era, the greatest effect was felt by the German Democratic Republic: the top performing economy in the Soviet bloc, but, like a twin child with a birth defect, weighed down by the perpetual burden of mismanagement and exploitation from East Berlin and Moscow. The economic gap between the two Germanys grew ever wider: wide and deep enough, eventually, to undermine the Berlin Wall.

As long ago as 1958, the Federal Republic took over Britain's position as the world's second largest exporter (after the US). Average living standards, measured by output per head, which had been 30 per cent below Britain's during the 1950s, surpassed those in the UK by 25 per cent by the end of the 1980s. Ironically, since output per head in united Germany dropped by around 15 per cent from previous levels in West Germany, unification virtually eliminated Germany's 'wealth differential' compared with the rest of the EC.[10]

During the initial post-war decades, the Bonn Finance Ministry won renown for fiscal policies as straightforward and orthodox as those of the Third Reich had been convoluted and reckless. The German-American banker Henry Wallich wrote in 1955:

Ten years ago Germany was a defeated and broken country, seemingly ruined beyond resurrection in our time. Today the West German economy is among the healthiest in Europe . . . Her public finances, with their succession of surpluses in the face of tax reductions, are the envy of Europe.[11]

The Bundesbank, the successor of the Bank deutscher Länder, established in 1948 under the control of the occupying powers, was given formal independence from government in 1957. It became a stern national repository of the determination never to permit a repetition of past inflationary excesses. The Bretton Woods system of fixed exchange rates underpinned German exports by maintaining the D-Mark – in spite of the two revaluations in 1961 and 1969 – at relatively undervalued levels on the world's foreign exchange markets.

The West German recovery provided an auspicious environment for expansion of the country's small and medium-sized businesses, the celebrated *Mittelstand*, and of its large joint-stock industrial companies and banks. Many of the latter had been founded during the golden age of manufacturing fecundity in the last thirty years of the nineteenth century. They had survived the lurching irresolution of the Weimar republic; they had endured – and sometimes abetted – the criminal truculence of Nazism; and they prospered anew as capitalist values were restored in the high-growth period of the Federal Republic. The large industrial groups, led by Daimler-Benz, Volkswagen and BMW in motor vehicles, the Siemens electrical conglomerate and the big three chemical companies BASF, Hoechst and Bayer, became the modern ambassadors of German power. The expansion of German companies abroad was a particular feature of the late 1980s and early 1990s, exemplified by Daimler-Benz's decision to start production in the US, the extension of Siemens and Volkswagen activities into central and eastern Europe and BMW's takeover of Britain's Rover car group. Of the twenty-one European companies in the world's top fifty industrial corporations at the beginning of the 1990s, seven were German, compared with five from France, three from Italy, and two each from Britain, the Netherlands and Switzerland.[12]

The premise behind Erhard's 'social market economy' was that liberal economic stewardship, combined with a controlled safety net for the underprivileged, would provide the best guarantee for social stability. As Alfred Müller-Armack, Erhard's long-time aide once put it, the aim was 'market freedom with social balance'. Robust anti-trust legislation ensured there would be no return to the corruptive embrace of the pre-war industrial cartels. Yet under post-war Germany's corporate capitalism, the play of market forces was never completely unfettered. This was reflected not only in the growth of the welfare state, expanding the pillars of the system laid down in the 1880s by Chancellor Otto von Bismarck, but also by the seriousness with which the government carried out its duty of providing an overall policy framework for economic growth. Under Erhard's orthodox economic doctrine of *Ordnungspolitik*, the government's credo was that industrial decision-making, as far as possible, should be left to industry. None the less, the big decisions were not infrequently taken after consultation with the government.

The breakdown of the Bretton Woods system in 1971-73, the big increase in international oil prices in autumn 1973, and increasing claims on welfare resources in a West German society that had become both more mature and more demanding, led to a sharp slowing down of economic expansion in the 1970s and 1980s. Annual growth rates fell from 8 per cent in 1951-60 and 4.5 per cent in 1961-70 to 2.7 per cent in 1971-80 and

2.3 per cent in 1981-90. At the same time, after 1973 Germany started to suffer a sharp underlying rise in unemployment. As in the rest of Europe, the number out of work ratcheted successively higher after each economic downturn.

In terms of the relative size of its economy, West Germany reached its zenith in 1970, when it accounted for 29 per cent of gross domestic product of the twelve countries that eventually made up the European Community. Nearly every year during the next two decades, West Germany's growth rate was below the average of its EC partners, so its share of overall EC output fell slightly over this time. In 1993, after the incorporation of East Germany, united Germany's share of the European Community's GDP was 28 per cent, lower than the percentage in 1970 made up by West Germany alone.[13]

Reflecting a fall in the EC's share of world output since the 1970s, Germany's relative decline on a worldwide basis was even greater. United Germany's share of world output in 1993 was about 7.5 per cent (against 27 per cent for the US and 16 per cent for Japan), while in 1970 West Germany itself made up 9 per cent of the world economy.[14] Those voicing concern in 1990-91 about united Germany's economic might were adopting far too narrow a perspective. In global terms, Germany's relative strength had already been declining for two decades.

III

As Germany confronted the direct consequences of unification, it had also to measure up to additional challenges resulting from sweeping change in the world economy. At the beginning of the 1990s, a central feature of the international march of free-market capitalism was the emergence of a fresh group of competitors from the newly industrialising world. The European nations that launched the manufacturing revolutions of the eighteenth and nineteenth centuries ceded industrial leadership to the US after the First World War. At the beginning of the 1990s, they faced the prospect of a renewed transfer in the balance of economic power – this time, towards the rapidly expanding economies of South East Asia and the Pacific Rim. The Asian 'tiger' countries, led by South Korea, Singapore, Hong Kong and Taiwan, had absorbed Japanese and US knowledge on modern industrial techniques. With tenacity, intelligence and labour costs only a fraction of those in Japan and the West, they had secured footholds on world markets for consumer products and industrial goods ranging from cutlery to aircraft.

Beyond Japan and the 'tigers', another economy was stirring, a giant accounting for one-fifth of the world's population. China's awakening had long been predicted; it would take over the position of the US as the world's 'greatest real community' as soon as its people learned to read, the writer H.G. Wells had predicted in 1922.[15] As it captured an increasing share of world investment and trade and targeted its manufacturing skills on goods that could be produced at labour costs of only 2 or 3 per cent of those in Europe,[16] China was approaching the end of its slumber.

During the 1980s, these world economic displacements were already starting to become apparent. Europe's initial slow recovery from the 1981-82 recession had strengthened anxiety that the European Community was falling irretrievably behind the US and Japan. The desire to cure the sapping disease dubbed 'Eurosclerosis' led to agreement in 1985 to step up free trade under the 'single market', enshrined in the Single European Act that took effect in 1987.

An optimistic report from the European Commission in 1988 predicted that, over the medium term, the 'single market' would increase the EC's output by 4.5 per cent.[17] It would also, according to the report's conclusions, dampen inflation, improve countries' budget positions, lower balance of payments deficits and create 1.8 million jobs. In fact, the economic impact of the 'single market' was most marked before it was properly established. In the late 1980s, many European companies speeded up investment through cross-border mergers and acquisitions to set up pan-European sales and production networks, in preparation for the formal start of the 'single market' at the end of 1992. This provided a significant fillip for EC economic growth, which spurted to an annual average of more than 3 per cent between 1986 and 1990 – the most buoyant five-year period for the EC economy since 1969-73, immediately before the 1973 oil price shock.

At the hub of Europe, West Germany gained particular advantage from this anticipatory economic stimulus towards the end of the 1980s. The Europe-wide 'single market' investment flurry reinforced the initial stimulus of the German unification process. The result was the unusual West German growth spurt between 1989 and 1991, when the economy grew at an annual average rate of 4 per cent – the highest since the 1960s.[18] For a time, the boom was self-feeding. This sudden flurry was, however, unsustainable, as were many of the economic policy illusions that accompanied it.

By the time the 'single market' formally came into effect, at the beginning of 1993, the European growth surge had given way to a recession in Germany and the rest of the continent.[19] However, the 'single market' provided a forceful impetus towards further European integration. By 1993, EC states and the European Free Trade Association (EFTA) – four of the members of which (Austria, Finland, Norway and Sweden) are due to join the EC in 1995 – carried out 70 per cent of their trade with each other. An average 20 per cent of each country's trade is with Europe's pivotal nation – Germany. Integration, however, can have negative side effects. The 1993 European downturn was aggravated by the strong interaction between the German economy and those of the rest of the continent. This emphasised one of the drawbacks of the 'single market' programme. By concentrating on liberalising internal rather than external trade, the EC has failed to exploit the full potential of expanding commerce with more dynamic regions such as South East Asia.

IV

Germany's 1989-91 'unity boom' raised expectations that Germany was about to experience another 1950s-style miracle. But it masked the persistence of structural deficiencies that had already been identified during the 1980s, and were then intensified by international competition. The drama and pathos of unification distracted the attention of policy-makers at a crucial juncture.

In the period between 1989 and 1994, the main failure of German economic policy was not, on the whole, one of inappropriate or insufficient diagnosis. When the Wall collapsed in November 1989, the country was unprepared. In the months afterwards, however, economists, business leaders and politicians put forward

well-argued analyses of the strains ahead. By 1992, after
the sharp downturn in the East German economy, few
Germans were unaware that they were embarking on a
supremely arduous transition. Rather, what was lacking
was the will and authority to take action to put the
country on to a sounder path. The fault did not lie
merely with the political leadership; it was woven into
the fabric of German society. A nation with an extreme
collective memory of past upheavals had grown allergic
to crises. When the bell of unity tolled, Germany lacked
sufficient strength and flexibility to answer the call.

Already towards the end of the 1980s, West Germany's difficulties in coping with worldwide competition
had become well-recognised. In 1988-89, the Federation of
German Industry (BDI) launched a campaign to improve
Germany's economic vigour. It used a slogan – *Standort
Deutschland* (Germany as a place to do business) –
which Kohl subsequently re-invented as his leitmotif
for the 1994 general election campaign. In 1989, Tyll
Necker, the BDI president and chairman of a thriving
agricultural machinery company in Schleswig-Holstein,
pleaded for cuts in corporation tax together with more
industry deregulation and job flexibility. Interviewed
in his Rhine-side office in Cologne in 1989, he said the
Federal Republic was benefiting from a buoyant phase
of European growth partly resulting from the 'single
market' programme. This would not last indefinitely,
he added:

> The sun will not shine for ever . . . If the inter-
> national economy weakens, we will have a situation
> where demand for our capital goods weakens. That is
> the vulnerability of the Federal Republic. We should
> repair the roof in time – during the good weather.[20]

Necker remained BDI president until 1990, and subsequently returned to the job two years after unification, in 1992.[21] One of Germany's few top industrialists who could express serious economic policy points in colourful and easily understood language, Necker promptly returned to the offensive by hitting out at excessive production costs, particularly in East Germany. Interviewed again in his Cologne office in 1993, Necker emphasised how Germany's principal competitive handicap – high labour costs – had been obscured during the post-unification upswing, and had now become fully visible. His meteorological metaphors were more sombre than in 1989. Otherwise, the message was strikingly unchanged:

> When the sun shines, you do not see the holes in the roof . . . Cyclical difficulties are temporary, like bad weather. But if we don't solve our structural problems, we face the risk of a climatic change, and perhaps an ice age.[22]

A comparison of Kohl's statements in 1989 and 1994 provides even stronger evidence of how Germany's leaders failed to heed their own warnings. Although keenly aware of the importance of providing the right psychological climate for entrepreneurs, Kohl has no detailed interest in economics. He does not regard this as a failing, but none the less registers intense aversion when critics point it out. In 1989, however, even Kohl was convinced that West Germany needed to improve its competitive structures to prepare for the rigours of the 'single market'. To make Germany 'fit' for the '1992 programme', Kohl stressed in February 1989 the urgent need for tough and unpopular reforms in the tax, pensions, telecommunications and health systems:

> Our problem is that we have prosperity today as never before. This prosperity has led to people becoming sated in some respects. Too many people think this will automatically continue into the future. My duty is sometimes to tell people unpleasant things and to say that we cannot go on like this.[23]

Kohl's logic was as insurmountable as his subsequent inability to follow his own advice was inexplicable. After five years of economic difficulties, in February 1994, in a speech at an industrial conference, the chancellor set down a series of recommendations for improving Germany's proficiency as an industrial base:

> We are not dealing with a normal recession, but with structural problems which have been mounting for a long time. These are problems of the old Federal Republic, which don't have anything to do with German unity. For decades, we have failed to carry out important reforms, for instance in the post and telecommunications field or in the railways . . . We have to change our mentality, go down new paths, become more flexible. Otherwise we will fall behind in international competition.[24]

Resorting to a familiar device for improving the intellectual quality of politicians' addresses to businessmen, Kohl's advisers inserted in his speech a judicious quotation from Goethe: 'Intent alone is not enough; we must pass to action.' Amid the ebb and flow of world events, Kohl had been preaching good intentions about economic reforms for five years. He was still trying to put them into effect.

V

During the travails of unity, Germany could turn to a supreme asset: an industrial calibre and culture fostered during more than a century of fluctuating economic fortunes. Between 1880 and the end of the 1980s, Britain's share of world export markets for manufactured goods fell from 38 per cent to 6 per cent. Germany's remained roughly unchanged at 15 per cent. The importance of manufacturing in the German economy is far higher than in other industrialised countries.[25] In the more competitive economic environment of the 1990s, Germany's challenge will be to expand its relatively under-developed service sector. As employment is inevitably reduced in internationally-exposed manufacturing industry, Germany's only chance to cushion the effect will be through a deregulatory drive permitting expansion of the service sector.

A vital part of West Germany's post-war success story has been the consensus-based organisation of industry – a pivotal part of the German 'model' of close contacts between management and trade unions, first established in the troubled aftermath of the First World War.[26] The interlocking system of German capitalism was built on networks of influence and like-mindedness linking representatives of capital, labour organisations and the government: 'a relationship of respect', as Edzard Reuter of Daimler-Benz put it.[27] During much of the post-war period, the West German system, with its emphasis on consultation and cooperation between the different sides of industry, seemed to offer a better functioning, more reliable and fairer means of achieving economic growth and distributing its rewards than freewheeling Anglo-Saxon capitalism. Although Germany's consensus culture still offered important benefits, its failure to respond adequately to economic realities during the unification saga represented a serious handicap.

In particular, the post-1989 period of faster economic expansion exposed the flaws of centralised, countrywide wage bargaining. At a time when Germany urgently needed to re-establish competitive advantage, wage rises in both East and West Germany ran well ahead of productivity, aggravating the 1992-93 recession and holding back subsequent prospects for export-led recovery. In the early 1990s, unification combined with worldwide deregulation subjected the German 'model' to deep-seated pressures. Although the priority given to consensus will survive, the 'model' has been forced to undergo its most significant modification since 1945.

One sign of the structural difficulties in the economy and the shift away from earlier priorities was the persistent growth of state subsidies from the 1970s onwards, particularly in coal mining and agriculture. Another was the change in the Economics Ministry itself, which after 1973 became increasingly focused on supporting traditional industries like shipbuilding or supporting new ones like aerospace, activities which neither led to successes, nor sat easily with the creed of free-market *Ordnungspolitik* fostered by Ludwig Erhard. A succession of economics ministers during the 1970s and 1980s lacked the firm touch of Erhard and the other main post-war economics minister, Karl Schiller. Five of their successors from 1977 onwards left the ministry under a cloud.

A third indication of underlying problems was the

sharp decline in foreign investment into West Germany in the 1980s and 1990s, combined with a sharp increase in German investment abroad – both illustrating the country's fading attractiveness for international business.[28] The trend reflected not only West Germany's high production costs, but also employers' unease about the rigidity of German labour markets, particularly the difficulty of laying off staff in the event of economic downturn. One side effect of falling foreign investment was to reduce West Germany's exposure to innovative foreign manufacturing and management techniques of the sort practised in Japan.

A fourth symptom of malaise was the general difficulty of encouraging entrepreneurial activities in a society which had become progressively attuned to comfort rather than to risk-taking. Germany shared with other European countries a general lack of success in new industrial areas such as computer technology, software and telecommunications. In the early 1990s, the main pivots of German industry remained vehicles, engineering and chemicals, as they had been for more than fifty years. Disappointingly, though not totally surprisingly, East Germany – in contrast to other former communist countries in central and eastern Europe – showed no propensity to produce a new generation of young entrepreneurs. Herbert Henzler, chairman of the McKinsey management consultants, believes the main barrier to improved economic performance lies in the German psyche. He berates a lack of innovation and dynamism:

> Not enough is coming out of our research centres. And we are not a nation that likes to establish new business. For an average young German business studies graduate, the idea of rolling up his sleeves,

1. The countdown to unification starts as East Germany's lifeblood drains away. East and West Berliners mingle at the Brandenburg Gate on 10 November 1989, a day after the fall of the Berlin Wall.

2. Eleven months later, Germany is reunited at midnight on 3 October 1990. On the Reichstag balcony in Berlin, left to right: Saarland premier Oskar Lafontaine, ex-Chancellor Willy Brandt, Foreign Minister Hans-Dietrich Genscher, Chancellor Helmut Kohl's wife Hannelore, Kohl, President Richard von Weizsäcker, East German Prime Minister Lothar de Maizière, Finance Minister Theo Waigel.

3. Europe's pivotal relationship, between France and Germany, takes new and constructive shape after the Second World War. President Charles de Gaulle (right) and Chancellor Konrad Adenauer attend a mass in the cathedral of Rheims, July 1962.

4. European Commission President Jacques Delors, whose plan for economic and monetary union was accelerated after German unification, pictured with Kohl in Munich, July 1992.

5. The Franco-German tandem gains momentum. President Valéry Giscard d'Estaing (left) and Chancellor Helmut Schmidt, co-architects of the European Monetary System, in July 1980.

6. Seventy years after the First World War, President François Mitterrand (left) and Chancellor Helmut Kohl take part in a poignant act of reconciliation on the battlefield of Verdun, September 1984.

7. Post-unity strains start to tell. Kohl and Mitterrand at a summit meeting in Mulhouse, May 1994.

8. Look back in understanding. Prime Minister Margaret Thatcher – for all her suspicion of Germany – got on well with Helmut Schmidt, seen here saying goodbye after a visit to Chequers, May 1981.

9. Kohl and Prime Minister John Major try to work out a direction for Europe at Chequers, June 1991.

10. President George Bush imbibes harmony during a Rhineside visit in May 1989, in which he hailed the Germans as 'partners in leadership'.

11. Kindred spirits. No hint of hostility as Thatcher greets Kohl for talks at Downing Street, April 1983.

12. Kohl on an election tour in Magdeburg in March 1990. A fortnight later, East Germany's first democratic elections produce a landslide vote in favour of the Christian Democrats and the D-Mark.

13. In May 1990, the D-Mark prepares to cross the Elbe. East German Finance Minister Walter Romberg (left) and Theo Waigel sign the treaty on German monetary union, watched by Kohl and de Maizière.

14. Three years before its demise, the German Democratic Republic appears to come of age. In September 1987, Kohl grits his teeth but greets East German leader Erich Honecker in Bonn with full military honours.

15. Soviet President Mikhail Gorbachev agrees that united Germany will be part of Nato, at a crucial meeting with Kohl and Genscher at Stavropol in the Caucasus, July 1990.

16. Under the watchful eyes of its neighbours, Germany must exude constant reassurance. During a visit to Poland in November 1989 interrupted by the fall of the Wall, Kohl embraces Polish Prime Minister Tadeusz Mazowiecki after celebrating mass at Krzyzova.

17. Bidding to follow in Willy Brandt's footsteps, Rudolf Scharping becomes chairman of the Opposition Social Democrats in June 1993. In the background, a portrait of the late SPD leader.

starting a business with his wife and possibly working himself to death is much too abstruse even to be considered.[29]

Under the new conditions created by reunification, in 1993 Tyll Necker of the Federation of German Industry went even further in his critique of Germany's love of economic regulation. He accused the government of imitating the communists by bringing in a new straitjacket of subsidies and market distortions east of the Elbe, in what he cruelly dubbed a second version of the old GDR economy.[30]

VI

During West Germany's period of slower economic growth after 1973, signs of management weakness in top German companies became more frequent. Some of these illustrated drawbacks in the peculiarly German system of corporate governance, which gives Germany's banks a central place in steering the economy. The network of German corporatism underwent a form of dynastic change, becoming less all-encompassing and also less sure-footed.

Through their large stakes in industry and their positions on supervisory boards, comprising representatives of both shareholders and labour, the big banks -- led by the Deutsche and Dresdner Banks – exert considerable influence over companies' affairs. The supervisory boards control long-term, strategic decision-making and decide key appointments on the management boards which are in charge of companies' day-to-day operations. The Deutsche Bank, which can lay justifiable claim to being Europe's most important and influential commercial bank, is synonymous with the main strengths – and some of the weaknesses – of German business.

The German 'universal banks', playing combined roles as lenders, traders in securities and long-term shareholders, have been described by one admiring UK banker as 'a bit like a combination of the National Westminster Bank, S.G. Warburg and the Prudential.'[31] These banks have shepherded German industry through a changeable century. The ability of German corporations to build up patient, long-term relationships with the banks and other large institutional shareholders, such as the country's big insurance companies greatly contributed to post-war success. German companies' relatively low dependence on stock market finance shielded them from the risk of hostile takeovers from stronger competitors, allowing them greater ease than competitors in the US, Britain or France to focus on a strategy of expansion. However, by the early 1990s, chinks in the system were becoming apparent after several cases in which failure of management supervision led to highly publicised corporate losses or, in extreme cases, financial collapse. Questions were starting to be asked about whether the relationship between the banks and industry was too cloying for Germany's economic health.

With some justification, German managers and bankers show great pride in the cohesive financial pacts holding together German big business. Alfred Herrhausen, the former 'speaker' of the management board of the Deutsche Bank (a position akin to chief executive), who was murdered by terrorists in 1989, called American-style takeover battles 'a wrong path'.[32] His successor, Hilmar Kopper, spoke scathingly of the 'financial acrobatics' of corporate adventurers like Hanson, the UK conglomerate, which geared its merger and acquisition operations to short-term movements in financial markets. In 1991, Kopper summed up the advantages of the German system as follows:

> For some companies in difficult phases of growth and restructuring, it can be very useful to have a stable shareholder who accompanies them benevolently through this phase – and who does not complain about the need to maximise profits or payouts every quarter.[33]

According to another member of the Deutsche Bank board, Ellen Schneider-Lenné, 'The company is seen as a combination of various interest groups whose goals have to be coordinated. The company's prime objective is doubtless to secure its survival over the long term. Alongside this, however, the long term interests of employees, customers, suppliers and the general public have to be taken into consideration.'[34]

The emphasis by German companies on goals beyond immediate increases in stock market value, and their insistence on serving a wider community of 'stakeholders' – including customers, suppliers and employees – is worthy of emulation by countries like Britain.[35] But German-style bank–industry relationships also display some sizeable shortcomings. Precisely because these relationships with the banks reduce the need of companies to take account of short-term fluctuations in business and product cycles, German-style corporatism can impair the ability of enterprises to react quickly to outside events. By drawing supervisory boards into too close and trusting a relationship with management, the system can shield companies from the salutary disciplines of the financial markets. Management boards can be given an imprudent amount of decision-making leeway – until something goes publicly wrong. Banks themselves can face intractable conflicts of interest when they are both shareholders and creditors of companies that run into economic difficulties.

Furthermore, the role of the banks in the corporate ownership structure can be seen as a weakness rather than a strength in Germany's industrial system. Many of the banks' shareholdings stem from transactions in which the banks were required to support companies in distress during periods of economic hardship (including the 1920s and 1930s). The banks' equity stakes persisted in subsequent years because of the lack of alternative investors. Comparing Germany with the UK and US, the Deutsche Bank's Schneider-Lenné points out,

> The major difference in the system of corporate control relates not to the power of the banks but to the ownership structure of the industrial sector. First of all, we have relatively few listed domestic joint-stock companies, only 665 compared with 2,200 in the UK. Market capitalisation is only $430 billion (24 per cent of GDP) in Germany compared with $1,200 billion (127 per cent of GDP) in the UK. The bulk of German companies are small- and medium-sized companies in family ownership. Second, the ownership structure of our stock market-listed companies is different: 42 per cent of the shares are in the hands of other companies, 10 per cent are owned by the banks and 12 per cent by insurance companies. So we neither have many companies with broadly dispersed ownership, nor do we have a large weight of big institutional investors.[36]

A list of problems since the end of the 1970s – some involving the demise of celebrated companies that flourished during the years of the 'economic miracle' – underlined the potential flaws in the corporate system. AEG, the electricals giant, had to be rescued with a DM1 billion loan package from German banks in 1979, went bankrupt in 1982, and was acquired by Daimler-Benz in 1985. Krupp, the steel company, had to call on the Deutsche Bank's help on several occasions during the 1980s after failing to follow other steel companies in diversifying out of its core business. Grundig, once Germany's leading consumer electronics company, collapsed in the 1980s and was taken over by Philips.

The Klöckner trading group suffered sharp losses in oil trading in 1988, requiring it to be taken under the wing of the Deutsche Bank. Computer group Nixdorf, another company like Grundig which epitomised the 'miracle' years, but stumbled after the departure of its founder, was sold to Siemens at a bargain price in 1989 to rescue it from sudden heavy losses. Volkswagen, the car group, was badly hit by unauthorised foreign exchange deals in 1988.

In 1993-94, Metallgesellschaft, the metals group, averted financial collapse only after being hurriedly bailed out by its principal banks with a DM3.4 billion package, following revelations of large losses through unauthorised oil trading in the US. Deutsche Bank, the main bank involved in the Metallgesellschaft imbroglio, found itself in trouble again in April 1994 as the result of its more than DM1 billion in credits to the Schneider property group, which went bankrupt in Germany's most spectacular property collapse. Even Daimler-Benz, Europe's largest manufacturing company, encountered unusual difficulties as its government-sponsored takeover of the Messerschmitt-Bölkow-Blohm aircraft group turned sour amid the 1990s downturn in civil and military aerospace.

Many of these cases revealed failures in communication between supervisory and management boards. The effect was both to impede flows of adequate information on companies' looming difficulties and to hamper efforts to find solutions. The ambitious but risk-laden strategy of diversification into the electronics and aerospace fields pursued since the 1980s by Daimler-Benz, offered particular lessons. Deutsche Bank, which has had an important stake in the company since 1926, gave consistent backing for the objective of turning the motor company into an integrated technology group which could make use of maximum 'synergy' between its diverse high-tech sectors. Herrhausen, who before his death had been chairman of Daimler-Benz's supervisory board, was the main champion of the diversification strategy.

The aerospace plan was regarded with scepticism both within and outside the group, including by some members of the Deutsche Bank management board. Deutsche's patronage, however, enabled Daimler-Benz to push the plan through without exposing its shares to selling pressure. In the US or Britain, a company facing Daimler-Benz's strains would probably have been the object of a hostile takeover bid. In Germany, such an event would be unthinkable. However, with its structural problems worsened by high production costs and declining automobile markets at home and abroad, Daimler's difficulties became public knowledge in 1993-94 when the company announced a large programme of lay-offs, along with plans to transfer some production to lower-cost sites abroad.

This was a symbolic and a sensitive moment for Deutsche Bank to announce its intention gradually to lower its 28 per cent stake in the company. However, contrary to earlier expectations, Kopper continued as supervisory board chairman in 1995, thwarting the aim of Edzard Reuter to take his place. The relationship between Germany's Number One bank and its Number One industrial company goes to the heart of German capitalism. Yet both partners seem to agree that if the alliance were slightly less close, it might function a lot better.

VII

By 1994, a series of large question marks hung over Germany's economic future. Economic and social rigidities greatly impeded its ability to find the right answers. In a large number of policy fields, united Germany faces formidable problems. Looked at individually, none of these hurdles is more difficult than those confronting other European countries. Taken together, however, they represent large obstacles to Germany's future wellbeing. Because of Germany's pivotal economic and political importance, they pose quandaries with implications for the whole of Europe. The main hurdles are as follows:

• **High wages**

Wages in West German manufacturing industry in 1993 were the highest in the world at nearly $25 an hour, according to a list drawn up by the US investment bank Morgan Stanley. East German hourly wages ($17.30) were around $1 higher than in Japan, France or the US. By contrast, wage rates were $12 in Spain and the UK, $5 in Singapore, South Korea and Portugal and between $1 and $3 in Hungary, the Czech and Slovak republics and Poland.[37]

● **Lagging productivity**

Up to the mid- and late-1980s, high West German wages had been offset by higher productivity. After reunification, this stable relationship broke down. Between 1991 and 1993, wage costs per unit of production rose 13 per cent in West Germany, more than in the whole of the previous eight years between 1982 and 1990, and well in excess of rises in competitor nations such as Japan (4 per cent) or France (8.5 per cent).[38]

● **Higher D-Mark**

Between 1985 and 1993, below-average productivity gains and an appreciating D-Mark added to the increase in German unit labour costs expressed in a common currency. On this basis, West German labour costs in 1993 were 13 per cent higher than in 1991, and 40 per cent higher than in 1985.[39] The competitive position in East Germany was still worse. In 1993, East German unit labour costs were roughly 75 per cent higher than in West Germany, the highest in the world. Industry's cost position improved substantially in 1994, but there was a lot of ground to make up.

● **Short working hours**

One factor behind lagging productivity was the trend towards shorter working hours, particularly marked from the mid-1980s onwards. At the start of the 1990s, West German manufacturing employees worked on average 1,500 hours a year, compared with 1,620 in France, 1,630 in the UK, 1,850 in the US and 2,140 in Japan.[40] The trend towards shorter working hours is likely to continue. But, unlike during the 1980s, it will be accompanied by cuts in wages. This step will represent a means of reducing production costs rather than, as in the past, of improving workers' life styles.

• **Sluggish exports**

The rise in West Germany's habitual foreign trade surplus at the end of the 1980s reflected the relative weakness of domestic demand as well as an undervalued D-Mark. However, afterwards, export competitiveness weakened. According to the OECD, Germany's share of world exports fell from a peak of 13.1 per cent in 1987 to 10.7 per cent in 1993 – a sharper decline than for any other leading industrial country. The drop partly reflected West German companies' success in shifting sales towards the East German market. In 1994, German exports recovered much more quickly than expected – particularly as exporting companies at last started to draw real benefits from fast economic growth in the US and the Far East.

• **Low-cost competition from eastern Europe**

In the early 1990s, direct competition with the most advanced central and eastern European countries – Poland, the Czech and Slovak republics and Hungary – was held back as a result of EC trade barriers to imports of steel, chemicals, textiles and agricultural products. None the less, West Germany's imports from these countries in 1992 were between 65 and 165 per cent above levels in 1989. Overall imports were concentrated on consumer goods like clothes, textiles and shoes.

Because of big differences in production costs, many German companies started in 1990-91 to shift subcontracting work as well as their own production to cheaper sites in eastern Europe, by taking over existing companies or constructing new factories. A survey in the autumn of 1993 indicated that 30 per cent of German industrial companies intended during the next three years to transfer part of their production abroad, above all, to central and eastern Europe.[41]

● **Rising public debt**

Unification led to the creation of a number of additional government funding mechanisms to channel fiscal resources to East Germany. These included the German Unity Fund set up in 1990, the Treuhand agency and separate funds to handle the debt of the East German banking system, railways and housing authorities. The proliferation of these 'off-budget' accounts greatly complicated overall analysis of public sector accounts. The estimated end-1994 public sector debt figure of more than DM2 trillion results from consolidation of these accounts, an exercise adding DM500 billion to the official figure for overall government debt. The end-1994 figure is above the target of 60 per cent of gross domestic product set by the Maastricht treaty to determine EC countries' suitability for economic and monetary union. Even if public sector deficits fall after 1995 as economic growth recovers, the debt level as a percentage of GDP is likely to grow towards 70 per cent by the end of the 1990s. The German figure remains below the debt ratios in most other EC countries. Yet the deterioration in the debt picture in Germany since 1989 has been much greater than the EC average. The result will be higher taxes in Germany or higher interest rates or both.

● **Taxes and deficits**

After an initial delay in deciding upon tax increases to defray the costs of unification, from 1991 onwards the Kohl government implemented a series of measures to bring in extra government revenue. These tax increases failed to keep pace with overall rises in government spending, so both taxes and deficits rose during the 1990s. The biggest series of tax increases, totalling DM60 billion or 2 per cent of GDP, takes effect in 1994-95. Overall taxation will increase to 47 to 48 per cent of GDP, a larger proportion than that of any other big industrial country apart from - France – an important future burden on economic dynamism.

- Social security

Reflecting the effects of recession and reunification, government social security transfers in Germany, according to OECD figures, are estimated at 22 per cent of GDP in Germany in 1994, up from 15.2 per cent in 1990 – a much larger increase than in any other big industrialised country. As a percentage of GDP, social security spending in Germany is roughly 50 per cent higher than in the US, Britain, Australia and Canada, and 80 per cent higher than Japan. Among other European countries, only Finland (26.8 per cent), France (23.8 per cent), Belgium (22.7 per cent) record higher rates. The high cost of social contributions by employers has been one of the main factors restricting foreign investment in Germany and driving German corporate investment abroad.

- Technological innovation

Germany's main technological expertise is concentrated in its areas of traditional excellence like motor vehicles, engineering and chemicals – now suffering from intense international competition. Like other European countries, Germany has fallen behind the US in fields like computers, software, biotechnology and telecommunications. Figures from the Organisation for Economic Cooperation and Development show that Germany (like Japan) spends relatively low amounts on research and development in 'high-technology' industries, despite a generally high amount of R & D devoted to manufacturing.[42] Between 1970 and 1990, Germany's share of 'high technology' exports by OECD countries declined, with its main gains coming in the medium- and low- technology sectors.

● **Demography**

Germany faces the most serious ageing problem of any European country. The population will decline by about 15 million between 1993 and 2030. Whereas a fifth of the population in 1993 was 20 or younger and another fifth was 60 or over, by 2030 only 16 per cent will be under 20, 46 per cent will be between 20 and 60, and 38 per cent over 60.[43] The costs of financing pensions and social security for the elderly will be greater than elsewhere in Europe. During the fifty years between 1980 and 2030, these costs – expressed in terms of the sums needed per person of working age – will rise nearly 60 per cent in Germany, compared with a rise of 35 per cent in Italy, 30 per cent in France and 18 per cent in the UK, according to OECD estimates.[44]

The demographic picture contains one source of slight solace: the falling number of inhabitants could, in the long run, solve Germany's unemployment problems – above all in the East, where continued large-scale migration to West Germany, together with a sharp fall in the birth rate, has led to a further post-unification population decline.[45] Suffering from post-unity anxiety, the Germans are not about to celebrate nationhood with a baby boom. During the next twenty years, Germany will be Europe's land of light and shade: home to some of its fastest-growing regions, as well as to some of its worst unemployment black spots. Unification has bruised the most powerful economy in Europe. Neither the Germans nor their neighbours believe any longer in miracles.

Fear of Drifting

It may be very well to say that Germany is not an aggressive Power, but who can say when she may not become so? And that she may not some day . . . seek to unite within her boundaries the Russian-German provinces of the Baltics?

Napoleon III, Emperor of France, 1868[1]

Germany has a history both good and bad. It is a divided country. It faces the most serious security threat of any country in the Alliance. I'm like a psychiatrist who has to see a child from a broken home with complex problems. I take time with that child, and then I have to go back to Washington to explain it to the child's parents.

Richard Burt, US Ambassador to Bonn, 1987[2]

If anyone in Europe needs political union – with, as its largest component, economic and monetary union – it is we. On the threshold of the twenty-first century, Maastricht offers us the chance to escape from our position in the middle of Europe and to safeguard our long-term future. No one should lend his hand to wasting this chance. It may not come again.

Richard von Weizsäcker, President of Germany, 1992[3]

I

Germany's place in Europe is set by the coordinates of history and geography and power: a convoluted set of parameters. Since Germany's might in the past had been so comprehensively misused and the excessive side of its character put so outrageously on display, both characteristics, after the Second World War, were kept well out of sight. During four decades of partition, West Germany's overwhelming national interest was to prevent its new European and North American allies from thinking that it had one that was different from their own. The best method of keeping West Germany's hopes and ambitions in check was to ensure that they were never out of line with those of the rest of the continent. Channelled into a receptacle called Europe, they could become both dignified and benign: for Germany, an unusual combination.

In the treaty on European union agreed in 1991 at Maastricht, this fundamental tenet of post-war German policy was maintained and extended. German support for European union at and before the EC summit in the Netherlands partly reflected ingrained habit. More importantly, in 1990-91, it resulted from the requirement to provide reassurance – to the rest of Europe, ordinary

Germans and even to some members of the German government – that united Germany's future course would be reliable, predictable and safe. The motivation was understandable; but it set Europe on the wrong path.

The principal element of the Maastricht treaty was the plan for monetary union: to subsume the dominant D-Mark, the symbol and instrument of Germany's postwar prowess, into a single European currency, run by a supranational European central bank. The desire to constrain Germany's rediscovered power was turned into a central joist in Europe's future architecture. However, the framework was less strong than it looked, for it was held together by an incongruous blend of idealism and opportunism, bluff and subterfuge, suspicion and intrigue.

In their hearts, although they could not admit it, the Germans did not want European monetary union. Other countries, although they said they were in favour, were not ready for it. The European economy, although it looked resilient enough at the time, was badly damaged by attempts to bring it about. Europe's grand design suffered from grand design flaws. This was an idea whose time seemed to have come. In fact, as soon as it was launched, time started to ebb away from it.

The plan for European union was built on an illusion – on the fantasy that everyone would benefit. The European recession of the early 1990s cannot be blamed entirely on German unification; home-made errors, particularly in France and the UK, played a big part too. But mistakes in Bonn, coupled with the faulty response of the monetary union plan, levied a high price on the whole continent.

In May 1990, Kohl declared German unification would

'set free undreamt-of expansionary forces – here in Germany and in our partners in Europe and the world.'[4] Taking its line from Bonn's optimism about East German prospects, a European Commission document, drawn up in April 1990 to prepare for negotiations on East Germany's direct accession into the EC, exuded full-blooded confidence:

> In general terms we are likely to see vigorous economic growth in the German Democratic Republic, generating high demand throughout the Community, and an increase in imports from other member states. This additional growth will be reflected in additional [Community] revenue.[5]

In 1990, the Community as a whole indeed gained from German unification, as the fast-growing German economy absorbed sharply increased volumes of imports from its neighbours. By 1991, however, Europe was already starting to suffer from the aftermath. Germany became caught in a trap where economic setbacks on both sides of the Elbe generated increasing fiscal deficits – forcing the Bundesbank to maintain high interest rates for far longer than had been earlier expected. In view of the Bundesbank's pivotal role in determining European monetary policy, the impact extended well beyond Germany's borders.

The effect was compounded by the negotiations on monetary union that were carried out to prepare the Maastricht treaty. The EC locked itself into a fixed exchange rate straitjacket which severely hampered Europe's ability to adjust to the economic stresses of German unification. The correct response to unification would have been a D-Mark revaluation. By damping inflationary pressures in Germany, this would have obviated the need for drastic Bundsbank credit-tightening action. It would have allowed the other countries linked to the D-Mark in the European Monetary System to lower their interest rates – steps that were badly needed to revitalise their economies. In fact, no politician in Germany or abroad put forward a solution along these lines. Instead, currencies were effectively kept pegged during the crucial two years between 1990 and 1992, with the result that the full effect of the Bundesbank's tight monetary policies was transmitted through to the rest of the continent.

Henning Christophersen, the EC commissioner responsible for macroeconomic affairs, forecast in March 1990 that German unity would increase EC growth to 3.5 per cent in 1991 and 4 per cent in 1992.[6] In fact, the actual growth rates turned out to be 1.5 per cent and 1.1 per cent respectively. In 1993, EC economies contracted by 0.3 per cent – the first fall since 1975 – and only a restrained recovery was under way in 1994. The four-year stretch of subdued growth resembled the EC's previous period of economic doldrums between 1980 and 1983 – with the exception that EC unemployment in the early 1990s, at 18 million, was about 50 per cent higher than it had been a decade earlier. The European Community had expected German unification to produce an extended boom. Instead, it experienced something very close to bust.

II

When the Wall disappeared, Europe reappeared. The 1989-90 breakdown of communism brought into view the prospect of an eastwards-extended Community. Yet the

Maastricht treaty pointed in a different direction. For the Community to play a stabilising role in the East, most EC governments believed it had first to be made more robust and cohesive through acquisition of state-like power, in particular an economic and monetary union. However, the decision to give priority to deepening integration among the European Community's twelve existing members ended up weakening rather than enhancing their ability to open up to the East. One principal shortcoming concerned the EC's trade restrictions on imports from the newly democratic states of eastern and central Europe. The Community eased some of these controls in 1993.[7] But it continued to impede former communist countries' access to the western markets on which their economic revitalisation – and thus their eventual chances of joining the EC – so critically depended.

Conceived during the period of European division, negotiated when it was breaking down and ratified when it had ended, Maastricht was both the first treaty of the new Europe and the last treaty of the Cold War. Although it sealed the end of one era, it failed to find an adequate formula with which to open the new one. Many of its objectives were overambitious; most of its compromises, self-defeating. It went both too far, and not far enough. In mapping a route to economic and monetary union and to common policies on a wide variety of other matters ranging from foreign affairs and defence to immigration and industrial policy, it set itself too wide a variety of objectives. Because some governments had doubts about some of these aims, they were inevitably hedged with conditions which rendered them difficult, if not impossible, to accomplish.

The treaty, which came into effect in November 1993 after a long ratification process, provided EC members with a broad spread of measures to propel forward European union. It established:

- a new name for the Community – 'European Union' – even though the legal name for the twelve remained 'European Community';*
- the opportunity for joint decisions in social, technological and industrial policies, as well as health, education, environmental and consumer affairs;
- a larger say in running the Community for the European Parliament, in cooperation with the European Commission and Council of Ministers;
- the principle of subsidiarity, under which decision-making is carried out as closely as possible to the people whom it affects;
- common Community citizenship, giving EC citizens the right to vote in each others' local and European elections;
- a move to a common foreign and security policy, under which the Community would gain a distinct military role for the first time;
- a mechanism for better cooperation in police and home affairs matters, focusing particularly on immigration and cross-border crime;
- a timetable for economic and monetary union by 1999, based on targets for low inflation and restrained budget deficits among member states;
- a 'Cohesion Fund' to channel extra money to the four poorest members – Greece, Portugal, Ireland and Spain.

Foreign policy and defence matters, together with internal policy questions like immigration, were specified as areas to be treated through inter-governmental

* See note on p.xi.

negotiations rather than through new institutions – thus preserving individual countries' veto power. The so-called 'subsidiarity' principle – laying down that EC decisions should be taken as far as possible at the local level – was praiseworthy enough in terms of trying to make the EC more transparent and 'closer to the people'. But it was clearly at odds with the opposing requirement that certain important decisions – notably on the functioning of the 'single market' – had to be undertaken supranationally to ensure harmonisation of economic conditions across the Community.[18]

The most crucial area of decision-making elevated to the supranational level concerned the plan for economic and monetary union. This provided for the establishment of an independent European central bank to take over responsibility for monetary policy from national central banks. However, the EC failed to agree corresponding mechanisms for effective supranational control of other parts of economic policy – especially in the fiscal area, where budget policies would remain firmly in the hands of national governments.[9] This was a shortcoming subsequently assailed by German critics, primarily the Bundesbank, on the grounds that it created considerable potential for inflationary mismatch between monetary and fiscal policies.[10]

The Bundesbank's criticism had to be taken seriously. During the whole period that the economic and monetary union project was under review, Germany's own reunification-induced fiscal imbalances, putting constant upward pressure on German interest rates, provided a dramatic example of the strains on interest rates that could arise from budgetary profligacy. However, the German argument in favour of greater overall control of fiscal policy, while plausible, was impossible to satisfy. Supranational control of EC budget deficits would have required a pan-European government, or at least a decision to pool individual governments' power to tax and spend. This would have entailed a considerably greater abdication of sovereignty than that envisaged over the setting of interest rates. Neither Germany nor any of its main EC partners was willing to agree such a far-reaching step.

The Maastricht catalogue of muddle, miscalculation and contradiction was a long one. The politicians and functionaries who drew up the treaty underestimated the economic problems arising from the fusion of East and West Germany. They misjudged how the decision to set a fixed timetable for completing monetary union would create harmful exchange rate rigidities which would worsen the recession. They did not foresee that these extra economic burdens, shouldered at a time when Europe was already facing intensified world competition, would increase European electorates' reluctance to accept further dilution of national decision-making control.

The architects of Maastricht were also, it must be said, dogged by ill-fortune. The war in former Yugoslavia emphasised the gulf between the EC's objectives and its capacities. At the very moment that it provided itself with pretensions to a joint defence and security policy, the EC was confronted with an intractable conflict on its own doorstep. Failure to stop the killing in Bosnia did not simply lower the credibility of attempts to forge a joint foreign and security policy; it weakened faith in the EC's ability to carry out any policy at all. In 1992-93, this had a far-reaching effect on the electorate in Germany, closer to the Yugoslav fighting than any other EC member apart from Italy, more affected by flows of refugees from the war zone, and increasingly sceptical about the Maastricht blueprint for Europe, particularly the plan for monetary union. The conflict in the former Yugoslavia lowered further the German electorate's support for Bundeswehr peace-keeping operations outside Nato.[11] Additionally, it had an indirect effect on the monetary union project. If Europe could not stop a war, then – many Germans reasoned – it was hardly likely to be able to come up with a new form of European money that would be more stable and secure than the D-Mark.

III

Since the end of the 1980s, a confused debate about Germany's role in Europe had been emerging in German public opinion. Starting several years before unification, the German electorate's support for European unity had been falling, according to public opinion surveys.[12] Maastricht was designed to clear up this confusion by accommodating a larger Germany within a reinforced Community structure. Instead of providing answers, however, Maastricht brought into the open questions that had previously been barely aired. Far from offering the solution to Germany's European future, Maastricht became part of the problem.

Reunification heightened the German electorate's ambivalence about the traditional aim of a united Europe. Additionally, it accentuated anxieties about Germany's future course among many of its European neighbours and allies. There was a strange inconsistency to these worries: Europe was afraid of both German strength and German weakness. As one French journalist succinctly put it: 'The contradiction in French and European fears is that we fear Germany's economic dominance as much as a German economic crisis caused by the high cost of integrating East Germany.'[13]

Before reunification, Germany's policies towards the rest of Europe had been driven by a tactically adroit mix of good sense and good manners. In promoting close cooperation within a gradually expanded EC, West Germany during the post-war years had pursued several complementary objectives. Stable ties with the countries Germany had earlier intimidated or overrun represented, in moral and political terms, an end in itself, permitting the Germans to win freedom from the opprobium of the past, and respect as members of the international community. European integration provided markets for West Germany's goods and security for its people. It was even seen as a means – eventually – of bringing the two parts of the nation back together again: provided, of course, the neighbours agreed.

When Kohl was asked in February 1989, only nine months before the Wall fell, how he envisaged reunification one day actually happening, he could think of no more original a reply than that he wanted 'the political unity of Europe'.[14] The answer was illuminating only in that it was sincere. There was no national agenda for unification; Kohl was more preoccupied by Brussels than Berlin. Up to the end of the 1980s, the pattern of West Germany's relations with the rest of Europe had left little room to pose deeper questions on what Germany was, what Germany wanted and what Germany might become.[15] In conducting foreign policy, West Germany was required to do no more than anticipate and fulfil its neighbours' needs for a country that was conciliatory, stable and non-belligerent. German foreign policy was, in fact, defined by the absence of German policy.

As reunification loomed and was quickly consummated, these constraints changed. Germany emerged, once again, as a central European state – *the* central European state. None the less, it was vulnerable. Open mistrust by its neighbours could wound it; and, in 1990, mistrust of the Germans, previously voiced behind closed doors, burst into the open. It was a painful subject, but with typical forthrightness Kohl confronted it head on. Equally typically, he felt compelled to add that foreigners' uneasiness about German unification often represented resentment of Germany's economic proficiency:

> Sometimes there is more mistrust of the Germans than of other countries. There is some justification for this, in view of our history, and experiences with the Germans. But there are also other reasons, which have nothing to do with history, but reflect everyday economic envy between peoples.[16]

Other EC countries – particularly France and Britain – made little attempt to hide their anxiety that united Germany's European interests and priorities might sharply differ from those of the rest of the EC. After the upheavals of 1989-90, Warsaw, Prague and Budapest were reinstated on the mainstream political map; so, too, more ominously, was Berlin. In exchange for winning the partnership of the countries of central and eastern Europe, the West risked losing the partnership of Germany, or, at least, of the modest and self-effacing Germany to which it had grown accustomed.

France realised that, initially at least, German reunification would pose great economic difficulties.[17] But it seemed evident that Germany would eventually spread its reach throughout eastern Europe. In view of the country's centuries-long history of eastwards expansion, some of it peaceful but much of it bloody, the prospect of Germany enlarging its economic, cultural and political weight in this part of the continent was regarded with unease. At the same time, if its ties with the West weakened, there were fears (held, too, by many Germans) that Germany could experience a resurgence of an old and dangerous ambivalence about its place in Europe. Surrounded by watchful and jealous neighbours, the new Germany could fall prey to a similar mix of neurotic restlessness and recklessness that had plagued the old one in its seventy-four years of unity between 1871 and 1945.

Throughout and after the process of reunification, German politicians tried to counter fears of new disequilibrium by emphasising the unchanging strength of Germany's bonds to Nato and the EC. Hans-Dietrich Genscher repeated, with ritualistic solemnity, the phrase first made famous by Thomas Mann: 'Our aim is not a German Europe, but a European Germany.'[18] In the same vein, Klaus Kinkel, his successor, who took over as foreign minister in May 1992, declared, 'There is no alternative to the European path.'[19]

More often than not, however, such politicians habitually weakened their arguments by emphasising that Germany needed to be tied still more strongly to the West to avoid the danger that it would, after all, drift off on its own. The avowed policy of integration with the EC was accompanied by a sub-text: the threat that, in the absence of integration, Germany might after all turn away from the West. As Kohl's lieutenant Wolfgang Schäuble put it in 1993, 'If Europe is not integrated, our strong links with western Europe might weaken.'[20] Edzard Reuter of Daimler-Benz, the country's most high-profile industrialist, went even further when he spoke in 1994 about the danger that Germany might 'concentrate its economic energies on the East in order to form a bloc against the West.'[21] In September 1994, a controversial discussion document from the governing Christian Democratic Union and Christian Social Union in the Bundestag spelled out in particularly painful terms the need for Germany to be 'anchored' in the West: 'Never again must there be a destabilising vacuum of power in central Europe. If [west] European integration were not to progress, Germany might be called upon, or tempted by its own security constraints, to try to effect the stabilisation of Eastern Europe on its own and in the traditional way.'[22]

Could a nation with so little trust in its own ability to steer a steady course hope to find the trust of others? Ex-Chancellor Schmidt's view – perhaps overly pessimistic – was that it could not. 'I have no real confidence in the political constancy of our people.'[23] Schmidt set out a clear line of reasoning as to why Germany needed to be 'bound in' to the West through economic and monetary union. Unless the D-Mark was replaced by a single European currency, he said, the German currency by the year 2000 would be 'overwhelmingly strong'. This would make the Germans the 'masters' of the EC – a position which would eventually rebound on Germany by making it vulnerable to 'coalitions' of European states joining forces to curb its strength.[24]

German industrialists habitually play down their drive towards eastern Europe by pointing out with weary precision that Germany exports less to the whole of eastern Europe (including the ex-Soviet Union) than it does to Austria.[25] Statistics like this, however, serve to underline Germany's enormous potential for profitable trade with this region as it grows richer in coming decades – and as the D-Mark increasingly becomes the area's pivotal currency. Before 1939, in terms of per capita income, Czechoslovakia was a more wealthy country than Austria; the Czech republic may become so again. For corporate Germany, eastern Europe opens a new economic frontier. Six months after the Wall came down, Gert Becker, chairman of the Degussa chemicals group, admitted: 'The markets in the East are a temptation for us.'[26] It was just one of the many temptations from which, as reunification dawned, Germany's partners fervently hoped it would be delivered.

IV

France and Germany share the most substantial bilateral relationship in Europe. In the EC's response to unification, it was between Bonn and Paris that the most important – and most intriguing – tensions appeared. Margaret Thatcher's public demonstrations of *Angst* were far more excessive than anything put on display by the eminently better-controlled President Mitterrand. But the upheaval on the Franco-German trunk line was much more significant than that experienced on the secondary connection between London and Bonn.

France and Germany (like Britain and Germany) habitually underscore their differences through contrasting styles of public discourse. The disparities in political vocabulary during the reunification saga provided an accurate gauge of the gap in the two countries' attitudes and interests. While French politicians spoke of Germany's increased power, those in Germany talked about their country's greater responsibility.[27] While the French were preoccupied with 'disequilibrium', the Germans emphasised 'self-determination'. In December 1989, President Mitterrand warned against 'reconstituting a Europe in conflict' similar to the period before 1914.[28] Whereas the ever-sombre Mitterrand drew inspiration from the dark side of history, Kohl's vision was characteristically benevolent and bland: 'The Germans are being brought together in the spirit of freedom . . . not a threat, but a benefit for Europe.'[29]

Given the disparate standpoints of France and Germany, it was hardly surprising that their leaders made contrasting statements. What was novel was that, on a matter of overriding European importance, France and Germany had unambiguously opposing positions. For the first time in the post-war era, the Franco-German tandem became disconnected.

Just a week after the Wall fell, Edouard Balladur, the conservative French politician who became prime minister in 1993, illuminatingly described how the sands were shifting beneath Germany and Europe. As finance minister in 1986-88, during the first phase of 'cohabitation' between a conservative government and the socialist president, Balladur had already played a pivotal role in Franco-German monetary affairs.[30] His comment in November 1989 was all the more revealing for being delivered at a time when he held no government office. It was consequently shorn of any attempt at diplomatic obfuscation.

> One point is clear. The two Germanys will be united economically even more than today and union will be a powerful force of disequilibrium in their favour . . . Let us stop cultivating the illusion that, in the weeks

or maybe days ahead, we can bind the Federal Republic of Germany irreversibly into western Europe. Perhaps Germany will lend itself, in appearance, to this aim, but that will be only in appearance.[30]

As Balladur indicated, there were doubts over the viability of 'binding in' a larger Germany to the EC. But, as the countdown to unification accelerated in 1990, it seemed to Mitterrand and most of the French political establishment that this policy was the best – perhaps the only one – available to counter the danger of a return to instability.

Mitterrand knew that enacting this policy would not be easy. When he met Kohl for one of their innumerable bilateral summit meetings in Munich in September 1990, just a fortnight before Unity Day, the French president chose a decidedly laconic tone in which to salute united Germany's imminent rebirth. 'Good luck, Germany! Good luck, Europe! The outcome will be a happy one, if we desire and foresee it. Neither conflicts nor rivalries nor misunderstandings will be absent. Our path is strewn with this type of thing.'[32]

The attempted solution for 'anchoring' Germany – economic and monetary union – was a venerable objective that had preoccupied the Community on and off virtually ever since the promulgation of the Treaty of Rome in 1957.[33] The project agreed at Maastricht, indeed, marked the cumulation of efforts started during the mid-1980s to establish a single European currency as a means of improving the functioning of Europe's 'single market'. The Maastricht treaty thus saw the convergence of three strands of European policies. The aim laid down in the preamble to the Treaty of Rome of an 'ever-closer union' and the 'single market' process of the 1980s coalesced with and buttressed the new policy of restraining German power. Jacques Attali, Mitterrand's foreign affairs adviser during the 1980s, commented later that Maastricht was a long and highly complicated treaty with one essentially simple purpose: 'To get rid of the D-Mark'.[34]

Worrying about the Germans was one attribute that bridged the Left–Right gap in Paris. Mitterrand's conservative predecessor, Valéry Giscard d'Estaing, who together with Helmut Schmidt had been the main architect of the European Monetary System in 1979, gave a pithy resumé of the consensus view: 'We need an organised Europe to escape German domination.'[35] A man whose views on the desirability of monetary union were very close to Schmidt's, Giscard d'Estaing could hardly be accused of anti-German sentiment. Yet his remarks in April 1994 summed up the unchanging nature of the French desire for protection from Germany through a reinforced framework of EC cooperation.

Alain Juppé, appointed French foreign minister in the conservative Balladur government that came to power in April 1993, was in little doubt that a larger Germany embodied a larger potential for instability:

> Let us briefly picture the worst-case scenario, namely that the [European] structure bursts apart; we may not always have German leaders sufficiently resolved to anchor their country in Europe. If that should occur, some might perhaps think that a reunified Germany of some 80 million inhabitants, with extremely strong positions in central and eastern Europe, could recover its freedom.[36]

Juppé's choice of words was revealing. The prospect

of Germany recovering freedom of foreign policy action plainly offered its closest ally a perspective that was little short of nightmarish.

V

The Berlin Wall fell in November 1989 at a time when France held the temporary six-monthly presidency of the EC. As a result, the Paris government was well placed to marry progress towards German unification with its own long-standing desire for economic and monetary union. A committee of central bankers chaired by Jacques Delors, the European Commission president, had in 1989 set down a three-stage plan for progress towards monetary union,[37] although it prudently avoided establishing a timetable for putting it into effect. The objective of Emu was given strong backing, in theory at least, by the Bonn government, with Hans-Dietrich Genscher lending particular support.[38] The Bundesbank, however, voiced misgivings that became less discreet and more insistent as time went on.

European leaders meeting at a hastily convened dinner in Paris in November 1989 agreed (with the notable exception of Thatcher) that German reunification should accelerate European unification.[39] At their next regular summit gathering in Strasbourg in December 1989 – where Mitterrand was said to be 'rattled' by the pace of events in Germany[40] – EC leaders gave their basic assent to German unification. The condition was that it should take place 'in the perspective of European integration'.[41] In April 1990, Kohl underlined the link between German and European unity in a joint statement with Mitterrand asserting – implausibly and, it turned out, inaccurately – that economic and monetary union would 'become effective' on 1 January 1993.[42] The Franco-German pronouncement was worked out in secret between the chancellor's office and the Elysée Palace without the knowledge of the Bundesbank. The statement's chief significance was to provide a useful reminder that the chancellor had no great regard for the detail of timetables.[43]

A special gathering of EC government leaders in Dublin at the end of April 1990 agreed to integrate East Germany quickly and automatically into the European Community. Kohl gave the Dublin summit outcome whole-hearted approval: 'German unity is a catalyst for accelerating European integration.'[44] The Bundesbank, however, took a different view. Hans Tietmeyer, newly nominated as the central bank's vice president, preparing the ascent that would take him to the Bundesbank's helm in 1993, stated in 1991: 'German unity should not slow down the European unity process. But neither should it speed up the tempo of European monetary integration . . . United Germany has much to lose in the forthcoming reordering of European currencies, namely one of the most successful and best monetary constitutions in the world.'[45]

At the Maastricht summit conference in December 1991, Kohl agreed – pressed by the French and Italian governments – to set a timetable for turning monetary union into reality by 1997 or 1999. The plan, contained in a draft treaty drawn up after extensive preliminary discussions among EC government officials, was the centrepiece of a blueprint to disable the D-Mark. A discreet eve-of-summit dinner between President Mitterrand and Giulio Andreotti, the veteran Italian prime minister, confirmed the campaign tactics for the summit. As Andreotti admitted later, the ambush on the German currency was the result of careful planning. 'This preparation was the result of [our] personal contacts, as well as work by our officials. It wasn't improvised.'[46]

At Maastricht, the route to monetary union was agreed by eleven of the twelve EC governments. Britain negotiated an intricately worded waiver exempting it from automatic participation in 'stage three' of the move, the planned irrevocable fixing of currency rates in 1997 or 1999, which would be followed by establishment of a single European currency. The EC governments agreed that countries could participate in 'stage three' only if they fulfilled certain indicators of economic performance, known as the 'convergence criteria'.[47] These conditions had been drawn up, backed above all by the German and Dutch governments, to ensure that monetary union would be founded on the strictest of anti-inflation principles.

By the agreement on a route map towards political and economic union, Maastricht could be said to have conformed to a long-held German ambition.[48] However, by setting a date for the demise of the D-Mark, the treaty was also, from Bonn's point of view, a project for monetary self-emasculation. In 1991, Germany's vision of the Europe it wanted was still decreed primarily by its neighbours' fear of the Germany they did not want. The logic of European integration decreed that, because Germany was growing stronger, Europe needed to become more united. For Europe to become united, Germany, the strongest economy, had to relinquish power. To this end, it seemed reasonable to agree – subject to the 'convergence criteria' safeguards – to eliminate the monetary preponderance of the D-Mark and to turn the Bundesbank into a branch of the planned European central bank. United Germany's economic grip was deemed too strong for its own and its neighbours' good. As part of the act of regaining national sovereignty, the Germans had to agree to give it up again.

When the Maastricht treaty was agreed, not all of the political establishment in France voiced enthusiasm. Ex-Finance Minister Balladur declared his scepticism. In 1992, during his period in opposition, Balladur stated his preference for the EC to set up a common 'parallel' currency, operated alongside existing D-Marks, francs and pounds, rather than a 'single' currency, which he plainly saw as infringing French sovereignty.[49] Yet in August 1992, arguing for a 'Yes' vote in the French referendum on Maastricht (passed by a narrow majority the following month), Balladur made clear that he regarded the treaty as the principal instrument for ensuring a stable Germany.[50] A 'No' to Maastricht, he said, would pave the way for German domination:

> The rejection of the treaty will not give France more liberty; it will simply allow Germany to act as it desires, without taking heed of its neighbours or its partners, without being constrained by any set of common European rules in its role as a military, economic, financial and monetary power in the centre of the continent.[51]

An opinion poll immediately after the referendum indicated that 21 per cent of French people who had backed Maastricht voted for it because they believed, like Balladur, that it was the best way to counter German preponderance. Somewhat perversely, however, a large proportion of the French electorate took the opposing view that, if Maastricht was approved, Germany would end up with more power. Reflecting anxiety that a

Maastricht-style monetary union would inevitably fall under the sway of the Germans, 40 per cent of France's 'No' voters turned down the treaty because they believed the treaty would increase rather than reduce German dominance.[52]

This Gallic ambivalence over Maastricht was mirrored in the public debate on the other side of the Rhine. While nationalistic politicians in France worried that economic and monetary union would bring 'victory for the D-Mark', German newspapers started at the end of 1991 to voice the opposing fear that Maastricht would result in a humiliating German abandonment of their currency.[53] There was no doubt that France and Germany were locked in a long-term embrace; for their own good and that of Europe, both partners wanted to stick to it. Yet it was not one in which either country felt particularly comfortable. Reasons for mutual irritation were destined to grow.

VI

At the time of German unification, Kohl's declared aim was the creation of a 'United States of Europe'. The objective was repeated as part of the regular messages of reassurance. 'Our support for European integration contradicts all fears of a strengthening of nationalism. We are giving up sovereignty in favour of the political unification of Europe.'[54] The chancellor liked to remind listeners that the term had once been made famous by a celebrated British statesman.[55] 'Our goal is the creation of a united Europe – that which Winston Churchill in his famous Zurich speech in 1946 called "the United States of Europe".'[56]

Kohl's policy was in line with his own and his party's

instincts, but it was also transparently geared to winning favour abroad. Partly because of this, it grew increasingly unpopular at home. One top German Foreign Ministry official stated presciently at the December 1991 summit in Maastricht that the campaign against monetary union suddenly started by the German press to coincide with the meeting of EC heads of government was 'a time bomb which could explode under Kohl'.[57] To counter German unease that the future European currency would be less stable than the D-Mark, it was vital, this official added, that the site for the planned European central bank should be in Frankfurt – an objective that was eventually reached two years later.[58]

In December 1991, Karl Schiller, the former economics minister, publically urged that the monetary union plan should be postponed in favour of 'widening' the European Community towards the East. In the first of what would be a series of anti-Maastricht statements from influential economists and commentators, Schiller stated that the plan was 'the beginning of a bad bargain' and urged that Bonn should instead give priority to building up East Germany and helping Eastern Europe.[59]

In the days after the Maastricht conference, Theo Waigel, Kohl's finance minister, brushed aside the doubters with his habitual breeziness. His response showed how policies had been replaced by slogans in the top ranks of the Bonn government. 'Our stability policy has become the model and yardstick for the new Europe. We are exporting to Europe the essence of the D-Mark! . . . Germany is successful in equal measure in bringing about national and European unity – the fulfilment of our dual task.'[60]

Waigel's forced optimism fell on stony ground. As the

criticism of the Maastricht treaty suddenly flared up in the media, the EC's popularity in the opinion polls fell further. A survey in December 1991 indicated that only 10 per cent of Germans wanted a faster move towards a united Europe, compared with around 50 per cent in the period before 1988.[61] In a poll in March 1992, 42 per cent of respondents said they would reject the treaty if a referendum were held in Germany, against only 25 per cent saying they were in favour.[62] In September 1992, 17 per cent of respondents said EC membership brought Germany advantages, while 34 per cent mainly saw disadvantages.[63]

At the same time, the tide started to turn against the proponents of a federal Europe. In September 1992, 73 per cent of West Germans and 76 per cent of East Germans wanted Europe to remain 'an alliance of individual states', outnumbering by 5 to 1 those who said they wanted the EC to become 'a federally organised European state.' Still more significant was the opposition to monetary union: only 8 per cent of West Germans and 6 per cent of East Germans believed a future European currency would be as stable as the D-Mark.[64] The chancellor was well aware of this scepticism. He responded with a symbolically significant change in vocabulary. In 1993, Kohl declared: 'We want [European] political union, but we are not aiming for the "United States of Europe".' He said he would no longer use the term, on the grounds that it could be 'misunderstood'.[65]

There were several reasons for the Germans' increasing doubts over the Maastricht treaty, and the goal of Emu in particular.[66] First, France's interest in using Maastricht to quell German power was seized upon by commentators like Rudolf Augstein, publisher and founder of *Der Spiegel* magazine, who complained that Germany was being tied down 'like Gulliver'.[67]

Second, the Danish electorate's referendum vote against Maastricht in June 1992 had important repercussions in Germany. Although the Danish 'No' to Maastricht was overturned by another vote in May 1993 after modifications to the terms of Danish participation, including an exemption to Danish participation in monetary union, the two referendums helped stiffen opposition to Emu in Germany by showing that concern about the plan was shared by other nations. The rallying call to 'save the D-Mark' was taken up above all by German far Right parties.[68]

Third, German taxpayers realised that they would have to pay for a large share of the EC's efforts to help poorer members adapt the structure of their economies in preparation for monetary union. To finance aid for southern European states, Germany's EC budget contributions were already rising fast, at a time when the costs of German unification were turning out far larger than expected. The Bundesbank added to the controversy by publishing estimates showing that agreed additions to the EC's 'structural funds', together with the newly agreed 'cohesion fund' for poorer countries, would raise Germany's net contributions to the EC to around DM30 billion in 1997 from DM22 billion in 1992 and DM12 billion in 1990.[69]

Fourth, the potential interference of Brussels decision-making with the interests of the German *Länder* attracted increasingly critical attention. The voice of Bavaria, traditionally the strongest supporter of the devolution of power in Germany's federal structure, was particularly virulent. In a plea for slower European integration to preserve the sovereignty of the German *Länder*, Edmond Stoiber, the Bavarian prime minister, claimed, 'In a European federal state, Bavarian statehood would be completely removed.'[70]

Fifth, the Germans grew increasingly worried about the apparent agreement at Maastricht for an automatic transfer of monetary power away from the Bundesbank without adequate safeguards for the stability of the planned new European currency. In 1992, a well-publicised petition from sixty well-known economists – including the ubiquitous Karl Schiller – focused attention on the danger that the 'convergence criteria' could be softened to make monetary union into reality in 1999.[71]

In a Bundestag debate on the Maastricht treaty in December 1991, Kohl went out of his way to praise the 'irreversibility' of the move to monetary union.[72] Later, he was relieved to be able to stress that it was not really irreversible after all. Germany's Federal Constitutional Court ruled in October 1993 that the final decision on whether Germany would join monetary union would be made by the German parliament.

> Germany is not subordinating itself to an unclear and automatic mechanism towards monetary union which it cannot steer . . . The treaty opens the way to a further step-by-step integration of the European community of law which depends at every further step either on conditions which the parliament can now foresee or on further approval by the federal government, subject to influence from parliament.[73]

The Constitutional Court's judgement, by laying down

the primacy of parliament to approve or veto the route
agreed at Maastricht, gave Germany a monetary union
exemption clause equivalent to the one so laboriously
achieved by the British government in 1991. Although
it flatly contradicted Kohl's interpretation of the treaty
in December 1991, the Bonn government greeted the
ruling as successfully confirming its own policies.[74] The
German commitment to monetary union was starting
visibly to fade. Germany would have the final say on
whether or not monetary union went ahead - and it still
had several years to make up its mind.[75]

VII

Germany's waning support for Maastricht after 1991
coincided with a period of Europe-wide strains caused
by the Bundesbank's measures to squeeze inflation out
of Germany's overheated economy. The treaty, and the
general expectation that the Community was already
en route for monetary union, greatly contributed to
magnifying the disagreeable international consequences
of the Bundesbank's action. In an economically integrated continent, monetary pain crosses borders with
discomfiting speed. In 1991 many European countries
clung to the belief that they were in a preparatory stage
for fully-fledged monetary union. As a result members
of the European Monetary System were disinclined for
political reasons to seek a realignment of currency
parities. This reluctance was amplified by the Maastricht
treaty's controversial 'no realignment' rule which laid
down that ERM members should keep their parities
unchanged for two years before 'stage three' of Emu.[76]
The pattern of exchange rates was becoming increasingly out of line with reality; but no country wanted

to risk the adverse consequences of being the first to admit it.

Europe's political and economic cycles were seriously out of kelter. There was a fatal imbalance between European governments' all-consuming desire for currency stability, and their opposing need for lower interest rates. Most of Germany's partners had been affected by flagging economic growth from 1991 onwards – a full year before the downturn started in Germany. Germany tightened interest rates in 1991-92 just at the time when other countries most urgently wanted to ease them, but were prevented from doing so by the fear that such action would lead to a devaluation.

A modest D-Mark revaluation, or a widening of currency fluctuation margins, during this period, would have enabled other countries to operate monetary policies more in line with their own needs than with Germany's. They would have been under far less pressure to follow the Bundesbank's strict interest rate policies, and would have had more leeway to lower the cost of credit to help revitalise their economies. This would not have eliminated the European recession, but it would have made it shorter and shallower.

As it turned out, the Bundesbank's tightening led to a disproportionate economic squeeze for many European countries. Most EC members had succeeded in reducing their inflation rates to below German levels. But they were forced to import high nominal German interest rates that in real terms (allowing for their lower inflation rates) subjected borrowers outside Germany to a greater deflationary burden than that facing companies and individuals raising loans in Germany.[77] France, for instance, with an inflation rate half the German level, was punished for its virtue by having to face real interest rates that on occasion were double German levels. On the other hand, German financial markets gained from disarray elsewhere. The Bundesbank's firm monetary stance increased the long-term confidence of foreign investors in the stability of German government bonds. Coinciding with a vast build-up of liquid funds on the international financial markets, the result was an enormous inflow of international capital into German government securities in 1993. This brought a sharp fall in long-term German capital market rates which saved the Bonn government billions of D-Marks a year in interest payments on public debt.

The effect of the Bundesbank's policies on the rest of Europe was clearly deflationary. But neither the Bonn nor the French government showed any interest in making the EMS more flexible. The Bundesbank suggested a broad ERM realignment, including a D-Mark revaluation, in informal soundings with other central banks in 1990 and 1991, but failed to convince either its partners or Bonn that such action was necessary.[78]

The lack of any major EMS realignments during the period from 1987 onwards built up considerable pressure for currency adjustments. When political uncertainty over the future of the Maastricht process emerged after the Danish referendum 'No' in June 1992, these bottled-up pressures eventually came to the surface during twelve months of exceptional foreign exchange market turbulence between August 1992 and August 1993. Two bouts of unrest dented hopes that the EC could remain on the monetary union track. First, sterling and the lira were forced to leave the EMS exchange rate mechanism in September 1992. Second, after an even larger wave of foreign exchange speculation against the French franc in July–August 1993, ERM fluctuation bands – previously set for most currencies at 2.25 per cent – were widened to 15 per cent to protect the system from disruptive foreign exchange speculation. Although the EMS calmed down again afterwards, in the first year after the emergency widening of the fluctuation bands, EC governments were much too fearful of a resurgence of speculation to consider returning to the old narrow bands. Additionally, both Britain and Italy, exploiting the advantages of floating exchange rates, made no move to rejoin the ERM.

The unhappy story of Britain's twenty-three-month allegiance to the ERM between 1990 and 1992 illustrates the ill-effects both of the system's lack of flexibility and of a breakdown of communications between the British and German monetary authorities. When Britain joined the ERM in October 1990 more than eleven years after the European Monetary System had been established in 1979, the UK and German authorities served up in private an intriguing foretaste of the disagreement on exchange rates that would burst into the open two years later. On Friday, 5 October, Britain announced it would bring sterling into the ERM on the following Monday, at a central rate of around DM2.95. John Major, the British chancellor of the exchequer, had succeeded together with Sir Geoffrey Howe, the foreign secretary, in winning reluctant support for the ERM entry from Prime Minister Margaret Thatcher, who had previously been implacably opposed to the idea.[79] Major, who took over the premiership from Thatcher a month afterwards, telephoned Karl Otto Pöhl, the Bundesbank president, to tell him the news shortly before the official announcement at 4 p.m.[80] The phone call was designed to impart glad tidings, but Pöhl's reaction was less than enthusiastic. The exchange went along the following lines:

Major: We are coming in at DM2.95.
Pöhl: That is unrealistic. That is not possible.
Major: But it has been decided by the prime minister.
Pöhl: I don't care about your prime minister.

Throughout Britain's period within the ERM, the Bundesbank made no secret of its belief that sterling was overvalued at DM2.95. The Major–Pöhl conversation was never publicised, and the phone call was kept secret from the governor of the Bank of England.[81] However, when the UK – along with Italy – was forced out of the ERM on Black Wednesday, 16 September 1992, after massive selling pressure on sterling and the lira, British disagreement with the Bundesbank made headlines around the world.

Less than a fortnight earlier, on 5 September, Norman Lamont, Major's successor as Britain's chancellor of the exchequer, had failed to persuade Helmut Schlesinger, the new Bundesbank president, to reduce interest rates at an informal meeting of European finance ministers in the spa town of Bath in south-west England.[82] On 16 September, Schlesinger was immediately blamed by the British government for provoking the crisis, after he appeared to suggest in a newspaper interview that sterling might be overvalued.[83]

Intervention to support the pound on 16 September and the preceding days was estimated at about £16 billion – the largest ever amount of reserves deployed in one currency operation. Sterling's departure from the ERM was a colossal political humiliation. However, the outcome for the British economy was largely favourable.

By following what Lamont subsequently called 'a British economic policy and a British monetary policy,'[84] the Treasury was able to engineer a sharp cut in interest rates and subsequent recovery from recession. The effect on the government's credibility, however, was longer lasting. In the year before Black Wednesday, the policy option of leaving the ERM and cutting interest rates had been repeatedly and scornfully rejected by Major and Lamont as 'a quack's recipe' and 'fool's gold'.[85] The autumn 1992 U-turn wrought great damage to Major's prime ministerial authority from which he was never completely to recover.

Another dramatic policy reversal was undertaken nearly a year later by the French government, when ERM fluctuation bands were widened at an emergency meeting of EC finance ministers in Brussels on 1 August 1993. This followed a worldwide flurry of speculation against the franc in which the Bank of France was forced to spend about FFr300 billion to support its currency – more than twice the amount spent by the British at the time of Black Wednesday. On 30 July delegations from the German and French finance ministries and central banks had met secretly in Paris for hastily arranged talks on possible ways of saving the franc. As the meeting progressed, the tempers of both delegations grew increasingly strained. The Bank of France was at one stage selling $100 million a minute in foreign exchange in a vain effort to prevent the franc falling through its 'floor' level against the D-Mark in the ERM.

Again – as at the Bath meeting in September 1992 – Schlesinger, the Bundesbank president, stubbornly resisted any question of interest rate cuts to support the franc. In the words of Jacques de Larosière, the

Bank of France governor, who played a vital role in both the 30 July and the 1 August gatherings: 'It was like a Greek tragedy. All the characters were destined to play out a part. You couldn't really imagine that they would do anything else.'[86] Hans Tietmeyer, the Bundesbank vice-president, already designated as Schlesinger's successor, told a long-time colleague a few weeks later that the Bundesbank should have been more 'courageous' in easing its interest rates during the summer to help the franc. None the less, he added that it had become necessary to break 'illusions' about whether the Bundesbank would offer France an open-ended commitment automatically to stabilise the franc.[87]

In view of the strength of the Franco-German political alliance and France's good economic 'fundamentals' – particularly its success in reducing inflation to well below the German level – the Bundesbank had made far greater efforts to support the franc than during the September 1992 skirmish over sterling. In contrast to the position of sterling before the Black Wednesday episode, neither side believed there was any need to change the central parity of the franc against the D-Mark. In later months, stringent interest rate policies in Paris succeeded in bringing the franc back to its earlier D-Mark levels. However, Schlesinger's acerbic postmortem on the summer currency battle illustrated the wounds left by the episode. In trying to peg the franc against the D-Mark, the French, he said, had all the 'fundamentals' on their side – except credibility.[88]

VIII

The effective collapse of the exchange rate mechanism

in August 1993 sent a shudder through Franco-German relations. The drive towards European monetary union depended on a political consensus between the French and German goverments. The summer display of mis-understandings and bruised feelings cast doubt on whether this consensus was durable. It also made highly improbable the oft-mooted notion that France and Germany could sidestep the Maastricht treaty and move bilaterally to establish a single European currency in partnership with other members of the EMS 'hard core' like the Benelux countries. As the clouds over Europe's monetary future grew stormier, it appeared likely that if the continent was eventually going to have a single currency, it would be called the D-Mark.

One prominent problem for supporters of monetary union came about as an automatic consequence of the slowdown of the European economy. Weaker growth, by depressing tax revenues and increasing government payouts on unemployment benefit and social security, increased budget deficits in nearly all EC countries. As a result, only one EC country (Luxembourg) in 1993 fulfilled the two targets for public sector deficits and debt levels laid down under the Maastricht 'convergence criteria'.* Especially in view of the poor outlook for public finances in Germany, doubts deepened about whether a sufficient number of countries would meet the targets in 1997 or 1999 to make the Maastricht plan feasible. Some sceptics saw their misgivings confirmed that the 'convergence criteria' had been deliberately established at a level which was impossible to meet. According to Erik Hoffmeyer, governor of the Danish National Bank, 'I could imagine that the Germans said

* See Appendix III, p.223.

that they [the 'convergence criteria'] were necessary because they were impossible to fulfil.'[89]

The Bundesbank's customary reservations about Maastricht were expressed in progressively sharper language. Otmar Issing, the central bank's director responsible for economic affairs, said bluntly in January 1994 that the Maastricht road 'seems to be blocked by immense obstacles.'[90] Tietmeyer declared: 'It makes no sense permanently to speculate about the date at which monetary union could come into force.'[91] He pointed out that in 1993, ten of the twelve EC members had exceeded the convergence targets for budget deficits, while seven had failed to meet the objective for government debt levels. Somewhat ominously, he added that Germany itself would exceed the debt target in 1995.

The opposition Social Democratic Party, too, started to warn that the Maastricht monetary union plan might have to be postponed. Rudolf Scharping, the SPD's candidate for the chancellorship in the October 1994 elections, stated his wish that 'cooperation and integration in Europe should be continually deepened.' But he added:

> Stability is more important than timetables, and it could turn out – who can prophesy that now? – that some countries will fulfil the Maastricht criteria earlier, some later.[92]

In the past, German politicians' traditional strategy on Europe had been to stake claims on as wide a variety of objectives as possible. The electorate was asked to believe that deepening could occur at the same time as widening;[93] that German unification could take place at the same time as European unification;[94] and that the future European currency could be as stable as the D-Mark.[95] By 1994, accomplishing all these goals at once was no longer credible. There were increasing signs that one of France's long-term fears was about to be realised. Germany was starting to shift its priorities towards widening the EC to the East rather than concentrating exclusively on deepening it in the West.[96]

By 1994, France's own political and economic problems had greatly reduced its leverage over Germany's European policies. Extending the benefits of Community membership to states in central and eastern Europe, where living standards were only one third of the EC average, would be an expensive and arduous task that could be mastered only over a period of a decade or more.[97] Yet it was plainly a principal German objective; what was still more important was that it was an entirely justifiable one.[98] By 1994, after a supremely tortuous journey, Germany's long-term national interest was slowly starting to emerge. The future lay in moving Europe's centre of gravity towards the East.

Germany in the Europe to Come

In their own interest and that of their neighbours, the German people must find a safe and honourable place within the European Community. Strong ties of blood, sentiment and interest link the Germans in East and West. It would be a dangerous illusion to suppose that a vigorous nation nearly 70 million strong can remain divided indefinitely. So long as the Germans remain artificially divided, there can be no unity or stability in Europe.

Anthony Eden, British Foreign Secretary, 1954[1]

Germany experiences a sense of anguish, sometimes rage, prompted by its own uncertainty over its limitations, its unity, its political regime, its international role. To the whole continent, its destiny appears all the more disquieting because it remains indeterminate.

Charles de Gaulle, President of France, 1965[2]

It is up to the Germans whether their unity is a welcome motor to the drive for European unity, or a brake.

Vaclav Havel, President of Czechoslovakia, 1990[3]

I

The reappearance of the German nation has raised many questions, most of them still searching for answers. What kind of Germany would emerge: A political dwarf? A large Switzerland? An uncaged giant? A Fourth Reich? What kind of Germans would they become: Richer? Restless? Resentful? What sort of continent would they wish to see around them: A federal Europe? A wider Europe? A looser Europe? A German Europe?

German unification and its aftermath have occupied the attention and the imagination of the continent and the world. Yet the outcome has defied most predictions. Germany has fulfilled neither the brightest hopes nor the direst apprehensions expressed in 1989-90. The country is neither flourishing, as Helmut Kohl once forecast, nor dominant, as Margaret Thatcher once feared. The alarming prophecy by one of Germany's most forthright opponents of unity, the writer Günter Grass – 'Nothing would be gained except an alarming excess of power, swollen with the lust for more and more power'[4] – has not been realised. Neither has Hans-Dietrich Genscher's seraphic vision of a Germany diligently exercising its new-found responsibilities in pursuit of universal brotherhood.[5]

The Germans have not lived up to their own expectations, nor those invested in them by the world outside. Heinrich Heine once wrote of the Germans' 'realm of dreams'.[6] At the end of 1993, the historian Joachim Fest showed that some things have not changed: 'The Germans have always had difficulties with reality. They are much more at home in the free world of thoughts, a place that carries them away from the hard things of life.'[7]

Confused about their circumstances and their destiny, the Germans sow confusion in others. In the wake of their efforts two generations ago to impose their will on other populations, during the Cold War the Germans became a divided people, closed off behind borders made by others. They have now regained their own borders and their own sovereignty. Yet the Germans remain marked off from their neighbours by an unworldly provincialism that is incongruous in a nation so dependent on - the rest of the world. They can show a baffling inability to understand their own psychology. Foreign economists, for instance, showed far greater aptitude than German ones in analysing the challenges of reunification.

They are still divided, although in a different sense from before. Incorporation of economically ravaged East Germany has made the nation poorer than the former Federal Republic. This was a fact that many Germans refused to acknowledge when unity was forged. Reality struck home only afterwards. Germany was late, too, in awakening to the consequences of worldwide economic change and heightened competition from eastern Europe. This delay contributed to a succession of economic policy errors in 1990-91 – and to the arduous repercussions once Germany moved belatedly to correct them.

Through unification, Germany regained its integrity as a nation, but not yet the right to be regarded as a normal one. The burdens of history have diminished, but Germany is still not at ease with its past. A new generation of Germans has grown up who, understandably, do not wish to be reminded constantly of the Second World War. Precisely because fascism and communism have both been comprehensively discredited, they endure as yardsticks – for the Germans and for their neighbours – against which many aspects of contemporary life are judged. For a small minority of Germans disaffected by the rigours of transition, these failed doctrines can still inspire distorted hopes of salvation.

II

Germany's strengths and weaknesses lie close together. The Germans neither aspire to superpower status, nor are they likely to attain it. In the wake of unification, German government ministers on visits to Washington, Brussels or Paris stood up for Germany's national interests with greater forthrightness than before. But since the government has considerable difficulty making up its mind what these national interests are, they are communicated to the outside world through a blur of obfuscation. President Bush's flattering description – 'partners in leadership' – has started to look like wishful thinking.

The Germans are stronger than many would like them to be, yet more vulnerable than many think they are. Other countries show irritation when the Germans flex their muscles, for instance during Bonn's campaign in 1991 to give Croatia diplomatic recognition, or when the Bundesbank displays its influence over European interest rates. But these same countries also tend to be disturbed by Germany's weakness in failing to control post-unity budget deficits or to play an adequate role in international peace-keeping. Two post-Cold War conflicts, the wars in the Gulf and in former Yugoslavia, have illustrated how the new Germany's foreign policy – in contrast to that of the 1930s – is neither bellicose nor effective.

For a nation with a rich and tortured past, one extraordinarily positive feature of unification was the moderation with which it was accomplished. It took place virtually without bloodshed. There were few heroes, and fewer martyrs. The entry of the D-Mark at a time when East Germany was still a separate state, the introduction of West Germany's legal code and political system, and, most remarkably, the withdrawal of 380,000 Soviet soldiers from East Germany during the four years up to 1994 were carried out with orderliness and precision.

Unification unleashed neither undue creativity nor unusual energy, neither additional verve nor excessive nationalism. As elsewhere in Europe, the gap between governments and the governed has widened, and the electorate's trust in democratic institutions has diminished. Popular support for the *Volksparteien*, the Christian Democrats and the Social Democrats, has fallen to around the lowest level since the foundation of the Federal Republic. Yet the Germans remain disinclined to vote extremists into parliament, and the basic elements of the party system established in the 1950s have remained intact. The quality of German political leadership has declined since the 1970s. But the Germans' commitment to democracy and their acceptance of long cycles of coalition government have not changed.

The Germans in the early 1990s experienced outbreaks of xenophobic violence and a revival of far Right, neo-Nazi parties. These worrying symptoms have to be taken seriously, and combated with the full force of the law. Yet they are not, regrettably, markedly out of line with developments in many other European countries; in the same way, public worries abut rising crime and unemployment, or about pressures on the welfare state, are pan-European phenomena. There is no evidence of neo-Nazi groups gaining broad political support. Economic strains have not led to anything approaching the economic and social breakdown that spurred the rise of extremism during the Weimar Republic.

As East and West Germany gradually grow together, there will be pride at the accomplishments and despair at the afflictions along the path of coalescence. In rediscovering nationhood, the Germans have also rediscovered regional disparities. As competition within and outside Germany becomes more intense, renewed differences of economic perspective are opening up between north and south.

Most of all, Germany is gripped by the polarity of mutual resentment between East and West. Economic unification between East and West Germany will take fifteen to twenty years to complete. The social and psychological differences will persist beyond that time, since the damage wrought by four decades of malevolence in the East will take at least as long to repair. For many East Germans, the process of adaptation and convergence will take place smoothly, without distress. For others, it will never happen.

This fate seems especially likely to befall older people. Already twice, many have experienced the pain of disappointment, first under Hitler and then under communism. As a result of the dashed hopes of unification, some of the older generation of East Germans may endure a third form of betrayal.

In the economic sphere, Germany presents a picture more of fragility than of great strength. Massive government-funded efforts to support East German living standards and improve the economic infrastructure east of the Elbe have created a mountain of public sector debt. As a consequence, German interest rates and taxes will be higher in coming years than they would otherwise have been, a heavy burden on the performance and competitiveness of German companies. In steering the economy, the Bundesbank brought about a serious recession in 1992-93 as an unspoken part of its plan to reduce inflation: a reminder that, when economic disequilibrium has to be corrected, there are no miracle cures. Cutting state subsidies and trimming the borders of the welfare state, particularly in pensions and health care, will be pressing priorities throughout the 1990s.

Excessive wage rises during the 1989-91 unity boom underlined problems of inflexibility that greatly hampered industrial efficiency. Deep-seated defects have been revealed in Germany's much-vaunted structure of corporate management, especially in the networks of influence joining companies and banks. Some policy mistakes, for instance the overhasty monetary union with East Germany, were unavoidable. Others, such as the belated recognition of the need for tax rises and the failure to make necessary cuts in public spending to finance the tasks of unification, were the product of government complacency or foolishness. Others were thrust upon Germany through international pressure – above all, the Maastricht plan to abandon the D-Mark. The trials of unification exposed a wide gap between Germany's ability to diagnose its problems, and its capacity to take action to solve them.

Yet the 1992-93 recession was not a collapse; it even brought some positive side effects. It provided the impetus for German industry to take much-delayed action to bring its costs into line with foreign competitors. At the same time, by 1993-94, the financial transfers to the East started to bear fruit with the first signs of real recovery in the East German economy. Net flows of public sector funds to East Germany, totalling 5 per cent of West Germany's national income at the beginning of the 1990s, will bring long-term rewards, but the transfers will be needed over a far longer period than initially anticipated. Germany has undergone territorial enlargement. Yet, to escape high domestic production costs, many German companies are shifting manufacturing – and employment – to cheaper sites abroad. High costs, vigorous international competition and worldwide technological upheaval will make large-scale structural unemployment in West and East Germany unavoidable and durable.

Without the 1992-93 recession, necessary economic adjustments – changes in wage-bargaining behaviour and the move to more effective methods in companies' financial management – would not have come about. The interlocking structure of German capitalism, and the country's elaborate and expensive schemes of social protection, were essential components of stability after the Second World War. Both elements now have to be reformed. The German system of corporate and social consensus is designed to prevent crisis. Yet only through undergoing changes wrought by crisis can the system survive.

III

Two great struggles are in train: the rebuilding of Germany and the rebuilding of Europe. If Germany is in flux, the continent around it will be so too. Similarly, the consequences of any external disturbances – war or tyranny in the former Soviet Union, recession among its main western trade partners, population upheavals, migration pressure, accidents at nuclear power plants – feed through to Germany more surely and rapidly than to any other member of the European Community. Central and eastern Europe is becoming part of the West. Yet the economic and social divisions between East and West Germany provide a reflection and a reminder of the large disparities in the organisation of lives, economies and states throughout Europe. Germany is the focus and the mirror of a continent united in its disunity.

Germany's financial strength provides the means to help bridge the economic gap between the eastern and western parts of the nation. No such mechanism exists – nor is one desirable – to smooth out pan-European divergences. As more countries join the EC during the next decade, Europe will become still more interdependent. But the structures of European cooperation will also become looser, less ambitious and more diverse.

In 1869, Bismarck issued his celebrated call for patience about German unification with the words: 'We can advance our watches, but time passes no more quickly because of that.' For a long period in the 1970s and 1980s, when the Cold War appeared unthawable and East Germany impregnable, many West Germans appeared content to slow down or even stop their watches, in the belief (and sometimes the hope) that the day of reunification would never arrive. When, against all expectations, Germany came together again in 1990, Europe's politicians launched the Maastricht treaty: an effort to put forward the continent's clocks, in the hope that integration would accelerate.[8]

The hope was understandable but misguided. During the years of German division, a central feature of Germany's relations with its western partners had been their worries that it might, one day, be tempted to diminish its ties with them. Similar anxieties about a possible German drift away from the EC and Nato, expressed in different fashions by politicians, civil servants and industrialists in France, the UK and the US, came to the fore at the time of unification. To balance these concerns, Germany launched a programme of reassurance. Under the Maastricht treaty, Germany submitted to being 'bound in' to a more deeply integrated European Community, on the grounds that this would prevent unification becoming a risk either to Germany or its neighbours.

In fact, the belief that German and European unification could be achieved quickly, and in parallel, was unrealistic. Unification led to a smaller than anticipated increase in Germany's economic weight. Furthermore, Germany's inability to control its resultant economic problems, and the failure of the rest of Europe to react flexibly to them – particularly because of faulty management of Europe's monetary arrangements – magnified the pain of adjustment, both for Germany and its partners.

Germany has frequently declared it wants 'a European

Germany, not a German Europe'; that it wants to 'widen' and 'deepen' Europe at the same time; and that German and European unification will take place simultaneously. But nations, like individuals, that try to achieve everything often end up achieving nothing. Declarations of mere hope, unsupported either by the will or the action to put them into effect, can be not only implausible but also sanctimonious and dishonest. It is evident, for example, that, far from not wanting a 'German Europe', Germany wants its ideas – on social policy, on the environment, on the need to combat inflation or establish independent central banks, on the balance between 'widening' and 'deepening' – to be followed as closely as possible by its partners. This is a question less of power-play than of a curious form of political morality. The Germans genuinely believe that their ideas are in other people's (as well as their own) best interest. Germany's economic influence, for instance as the largest contributor to the EC budget, makes it likely that its voice will be heard.

Germany's greatest priority is to bring to fruition the process of national unification started in 1989-90. The concept embedded in the Maastricht treaty that both German unification and European unification could be completed over a six- to eight-year period was faulty, and has caused more problems than it has solved. As part of a necessary re-ordering of priorities, German leaders will have to admit that German unification will take precedence over European unification. Europe will not be united until Germany is united. This is a reflection not of German desire for dominance or assertiveness but of European political and economic realities.

Europe's greatest task is to spread and consolidate in the eastern half of the continent the prosperity and stability that has been established in the West. If it is to accomplish this objective, Europe needs policies based on reality, not on false goals, false perceptions and false fears.

IV

Europe stands at a crucial juncture. The objectives of the European Community have become more disparate, more controversial and more important. Disparate, because the EC has started to shift its focus away from deepening cooperation among its present membership to widening it with the East. Controversial, because many of the EC's aims as laid down in the Maastricht treaty have aroused considerable public hostility in EC member states. Important, because EC membership is the main hope for future prosperity and stability in the central and eastern European countries formerly separated from the West. What sort of Europe will we see by 1999? A relatively optimistic, but none the less practicable, assessment for Germany and the rest of the continent would run as follows:

● At the centre of Europe, Germany will have recovered from the initial aftershocks of unity. Even after several years of fast growth in the East, another decade will be needed for East Germany's overall economic performance to approach that of the West.

● Modest economic recovery in West Germany will have been achieved at the cost of stagnating living standards and high unemployment. The registered total of people without jobs in both parts of Germany will have declined only slowly to below 4 million throughout the 1990s, although the shrinking population in East Germany will have reduced the acuteness of the unemployment problem there.

- The coalition government in place in its new administrative headquarters in Berlin, will have adopted the electoral slogan that Germany is 'part of Europe'. But the emphasis will have changed towards a policy of far greater cooperation with countries to the East.

- The EC's commitment to political and economic cooperation will remain, but a system of exemptions – ranging from monetary, industrial and social policies to defence – will ensure that the level of integration depends on the preferences of member states. Barriers to movement of people, goods, services and ideas within the EC will have progressively fallen, but the Community will have maintained an open stance in its relations with the rest of the world.

- As a result of budgetary constraints in Germany, Britain and France, the EC will have decided deep-seated reforms of spending on agriculture and regional aid, in spite of bitter opposition from Spain, Portugal and the regions of southern Italy.

- A streamlined European Commission, headed by a president and ten commissioners, will fulfil a mainly executive role carrying out decisions made by the European Council of Ministers, supervised by a European parliament with expanded powers. A second European chamber, made up of representatives of EC parliaments, will check the need for and scope of Europe-wide legislation.

- Although commercial links between the US and Europe will remain strong, the US administration will have made clear that its main economic priorities are towards South East Asia (particularly China) and Latin America.

- The US and the EC will have put into effect more effective coordination of military activities, through the establishment of joint rapid deployment units under the aegis of the United Nations, for peace-keeping in world trouble spots. German troops will participate in these units, although the German presence in missions in the Ukraine and the Balkans will continue to cause controversy in the Bundestag.

•   Following the accession of the Nordic states, Austria and, belatedly, Switzerland, the EC will be preparing to admit Poland, Hungary and the Czech republic in January 2000. Long transition periods will have been negotiated to restrict these states' access to EC agricultural aid during their first decade of membership.

•   The EC will have growing trade ties with Russia, but these will have little effect in countering the country's impoverishment and encouraging genuine economic reform. Any question of admitting Russia to the EC, even as an associate member, will have been put on hold as a result of the suspension of democracy in that country in the latter part of the 1990s. EC aid to Moscow will have been frozen to protest against the reimposition of authoritarian rule.

•   In spite of strong opposition from Moscow, Nato will have admitted the states of central and eastern Europe as associate members. The US military presence in Europe will have been cut back to no more than a few bases in Britain, Germany, Italy and Spain. European Nato armies will be organised increasingly through integrated brigades combining units from several different countries.

•   Plans for European economic and monetary union by 1999 will have been postponed. The Bundesbank will remain in charge of Germany's monetary arrangements. A number of like-minded countries – Belgium,

Luxembourg, the Netherlands, Switzerland, Sweden, Austria, Hungary and the Czech republic – will form a monetary area with their currencies linked to the D-Mark. France and Britain will be closely associated with this D-Mark zone.

• An EC ministerial meeting will take place at the end of 1999 to prepare for economic and monetary union by the new target date of 2005. Meanwhile, plans will be laid for the D-Mark to become the single currency for the D-Mark zone by 2000-02. The central bank for this currency area will be the Bundesbank, with representatives of other countries' central banks participating in policy-making discussions in Frankfurt.

V

Having made a unique and exemplary post-war recovery as a country cleaved in two, Germany has been navigating a unique and less than exemplary passage as a reunited nation. Germany's task, for its own good and that of the rest of Europe, is to maintain and extend its post-Second World War achievements of parliamentary democracy, social consensus and economic liberalism. To accomplish this, Germany and its European partners must show each other more solidarity and understanding than was displayed in the first five years after the fall of the Berlin Wall. The Germans have emerged from the Cold War, but they have not yet found warmth. They have striven mightily for economic growth, but their chief goal now is to gain the unqualified confidence of others. They will succeed only if they inspire it amongst themselves.

A prerequisite for an effective and self-confident Europe is an effective and self-confident Germany with the ability to set the EC agenda along with its main European partners, France and Britain. It is vital that these three countries should form a mutually supportive triangular relationship, so that the UK's ties with both France and Germany match the traditional strength of Germany's post-war links with France. Without such a structure, Europe will again be riven by national strife and fragmentation. The continent would be unable to master the challenges of dealing with a renascent, authoritarian Russia and with a US which, while remaining the world's sole superpower, will plainly be concentrating its foreign and economic policy priorities in the Pacific Rim and Latin America. If, on the other hand, Germany, Britain and France can discover a new basis for partnership, free of misguided hopes and fears, the chances will greatly improve that Europe will remain a vigorous, prosperous and outward-looking continent in the twenty-first century.

Notes

Chapter 1: Europe's Heartbeat

1. Speech at first ministerial meeting on German unification, Bonn, 5.5.90.
2. Interview with author in Cologne, 12.3.93.
3. Schmidt, *Handeln für Deutschland*, 1993, p.246.
4. The 1993 report from the Bonn council of independent economic advisers estimated overall public spending on East Germany at DM248 billion. After subtraction of East German tax receipts, this produced a net figure for transfers to the East of DM148 billion. *Sachverständigenrat*, p.151. The Bonn government gave a slightly lower figure of net transfers to East Germany for 1993 of DM138 billion. *Leistungsbilanz der Bundesregierung für die Neuen Bundesländer*, 1994.
5. Allensbach poll showing 22 per cent of West Germans and 11 per cent of East Germans termed themselves 'together as Germans'. Seventy-one per cent of those in the West, and 85 per cent in the East said they had 'opposing interests'. *Frankfurter Allgemeine Zeitung*, 19.5.93. For the most comprehensive poll on East Germans' reaction to unification, see survey by Infratest Burke Berlin, *Die Zeit*, 1.10.93.
6. The original Svengali, in the novel *Trilby* by George du Maurier, was a musician of Austro-German descent with the power to exert a mesmeric attraction over the heroine of the novel, akin to Genscher's hold over the German political scene. 'And you shall see nothing,

hear nothing, think of nothing but Svengali, Svengali, Svengali.'

7. Genscher: speech to the United Nations, New York, 26.9.90. Kohl: speech to the Bundestag, Berlin, 4.10.90.
8. Professor Laszlo Csaba of the Hungarian Institute for Economics, Market Research and Informatics. Interview with author in Budapest, 19.1.94.
9. Speech to the Christian Democratic Union (CDU) party congress, Hamburg, 1.10.90.
10. Speech in Berlin, 19.1.89.
11. The discussion on *Standort Deutschland* (Germany as an industrial base) was started by the Federation of German Industry (BDI) in 1988. The subject rose again to public consciousness in 1993–94.
12. Speech in Düsseldorf, 20.4.88.
13. The term used was *Anschubfinanzierung*. See chapter 3.
14. For the whole of Germany, national income per head of the population fell to just above the Community average. European statistics office (Eurostat), January 1994.
15. Michael Mertes, the head of Chancellor Kohl's speechwriting department, delivered a thoughtful exposition on this question in Washington, 1.2.94. 'I find it . . . difficult to understand how a country like Germany, so much depending on what happens in its international environment, can afford to be so preoccupied with metaphysical questions such as the problem of its own identity. I would find a debate on what united Germany's interests are, and how she could responsibly use the power she bashfully denies, much more exciting.'

Chapter 2: The Melting of the Ice

1. Speech marking entry into force of the Bonn Convention (*Deutschlandvertrag*), Bonn, 5.5.55.
2. Speech commemorating 40th anniversary of East Germany, Berlin, 6.10.89.
3. Interview in *Die Zeit*, 11.5.90.
4. *Grundgesetz*, 1949, preamble.

5. *Random House Dictionary of the English Language*, 1987.
6. Mike Dennis, *German Democratic Republic: Politics, Economics and Society*, 1988.
7. A series of Allensbach opinion polls indicated declining belief in reunification before 1989. Only 7 per cent of the West German population indicated they would live to see reunification when polled in December 1986, against 23 per cent in September 1989 and 51 per cent in December 1989. Even after the fall of the Wall, however, considerable scepticism remained. Of the 43 per cent of West Germans who said in a separate poll in December 1989 that reunification would definitely take place, only 11 per cent foresaw this occurring within one year. Most respondents believed it would take place, if at all, after four years.
8. Interview with author in London, 30.3.90.
9. According to Allensbach, even though very few West Germans believed they would live to see reunification, the proportion of the population in favour of unity remained fairly constant at 50 to 60 per cent in the 1970s and 1980s.
10. In February 1989, asked why he no longer used *Wiedervereinigung* (reunification) to describe the goal of unity, Kohl said he preferred the phrase *Einheit der Nation* (unity of the nation). 'Under *Wiedervereinigung* one understood something else, the attachment of the GDR [East Germany] to the Federal Republic . . . The idea – the vision – is that we want the political unity of Europe.' Interview with author in Bonn, 7.2.89.
11. Press conference in Moscow, 26.10.88.
12. Interview with author in Bonn, 17.12.90.
13. The volume of Marshall aid was psychologically important, but its absolute size is sometimes exaggerated. It accounted for about 1.4 per cent of West Germany's gross national product in the immediate post-war years.
14. West Germany successfully resisted having to choose between alternative US- and European-based systems for its political and economic development: 'Instead of choosing, West Germany has enjoyed the best of both.' David

Calleo, *The German Problem Reconsidered*, 1978.

15. Speech in Stuttgart, 6.1.46.
16. Speech in New York, 16.11.87.
17. Chancellors Brandt, Schmidt and Kohl, during private and official visits to East Germany during the years of division, were given fulsome receptions by East German crowds. This may have strengthened their own commitment to East Germany, but it also increased caution about raising unrealistic expectations. See for example, Brandt's description of his visit to East Germany in 1970. 'I would be back in Bonn the next day. Could I be sure that my influence would reach those who, because of their demonstration of friendliness, could come into conflict with a state authority ill-disposed to this sentiment?' Brandt, *Erinnerungen*, 1989, p.226.
18. Conversation with author in Münster, 21.11.88.
19. This view was held in particular by Wolfgang Schäuble, interior minister in Bonn at the time of unification. Also noteworthy is the warning by Claus Duisberg, a senior official responsible for East–West German relations in the Bonn chancellery, that an over-rapid move to reform by East Germany would spark the danger of intervention by the Red Army. Conversation with author in Bonn, 6.11.89.
20. Interview with author in Bonn, 20.1.88.
21. Comment to author in Bonn in 1990 by Peter Hartmann, then deputy director of Kohl's foreign policy department, later his security adviser and (from 1993) Germany's ambassador to London.
22. In 1993, Kohl said that if he had raised taxes in 1990, he would have been blamed for ruining economic recovery. Interview with author in Bonn, 26.10.93.
23. According to an Emnid poll in November 1989, 75 per cent of West Germans said they were ready to help East Germany financially, as long as this did not lead to higher taxes. In an Allensbach poll in February 1990, 75 per cent of West Germans believed that 'significant tax increases' were likely. In another poll, in October 1990, 65 per cent classified as 'not very large' the readiness of

West Germans to make sacrifices for the East.

24. Speech at Unity Day ceremony in Berlin, 3.10.90.
25. Stürmer, 'The Do's and Don'ts of *Deutschlandpolitik*', in *Aspects of the German Question*, Konrad-Adenauer-Stiftung, ed. Peter Weilemann, 1985.
26. For instance, at the Anglo-German Königswinter conference in 1986, where British participants showed considerable impatience over the lack of German preparedness for unification.
27. Conversation between Honecker and Brezhnev on 28.7.70. Timothy Garton Ash, *In Europe's Name*, 1993, p.77.
28. Calculation of the relative size of these transfers depends on the exchange rate used. For one estimate of East–West German transfers, see Jeffrey H. Michel, 'Economic Exchanges Specific to the Two German States', in *Studies in Comparative Communism*, University of Southern California, spring 1987.
29. Buying prisoners gave East German intermediaries opportunities for corruption, shown by men like Wolfgang Vogel and Alexander Schalck-Golodkowski, two of East Berlin's highest ranking figures in interchanges between East and West.
30. Ludwig Rehlinger, state secretary at Ministry for Intra-German Relations. Interview with author in Bonn, 10.3.88.
31. Interview with author in Bonn, 8.7.88.
32. Bahr's theme was in strict opposition to Kohl's policy that unification was consistent with EC and Nato membership.
33. Up to the fall of the Wall, Franz Schönhuber, the leader of the far Right Republicans, repeatedly stated that the Federal Republic's links with the West precluded reunification.
34. One acquaintance known to both Kohl and Honecker was the head of a local youth hostel. Reflecting their common geographical roots, Kohl and Honecker both understood the regional dialect from Kohl's native Rhineland-Palatinate. When they met for the first time in 1984 at

a government guest-house in Moscow for the funeral of Soviet leader Yuri Andropov, Kohl suggested that they converse in dialect for five minutes to prevent the eavesdropping KGB from understanding what they were saying. Interview with author in Bonn, 17.12.90.

35. For instance, the East German agreement to dismantle mines as part of a DM1 billion credit deal agreed with Franz Josef Strauss, the Bavarian prime minister in 1983.

36. Statement on East German radio, 19.8.89.

37. East Germany's fear of Gorbachev's new ideas was most vividly illustrated by its decision in 1988 to ban the import of the Soviet magazine *Sputnik* on the grounds that it contained subversive material.

38. Report to the Central Committee, 1986.

39. Comment in 1988.

40. Document written on 16.10.89 by the Politburo's 'balance of payments working party' for Günter Mittag, the Politburo's economic chief. Published in *Frankfurter Allgemeine Zeitung*, 15.4.92. The memorandum warned that East Germany's foreign debt was more than DM30 billion, with annual new borrowing put at between DM8 billion and DM10 billion. Exports to the West of DM24 billion a year would be required within the next five years. 'Otherwise, in view of estimated resources, our republic's ability to discharge its [foreign] payments can in no way be guaranteed.' Among the signatories to the document were Gerhard Schürer, head of the planning commission, Gerhard Beil, foreign trade minister, and Alexander Schalck-Golodkowski, head of the government's shadowy 'commercial' department. This explains why Mittag, in post-unity interviews, admitted that East Germany was heading towards 'an economic catastrophe with unforeseeable social consequences.' See *Der Spiegel*, Number 37, 1991.

41. Speech in the Bundestag, 27.4.89.

42. For an account of the opening of the Wall, see M. E. Sarotte in 'Elite Intransigence and the End of the Berlin Wall', *German Politics*, August 1993.

43. In an opinion poll carried out for the Konrad Adenauer Foundation in April 1990, 62 per cent of Germans forecast in the short term 'a growing fear abroad of a too powerful Germany.' A total of 58 per cent foresaw long-term fear too. Hans-Joachim Veen: 'The First All-German Elections', in *Parties and Party Systems in the New Germany*, 1993.

44. Article 7 of the treaty, signed in 1952, became effective in 1955.

45. Grosser, *Mein Deutschland*, 1993, p.11. The West had most forcefully advocated reunification when international politics ruled it out. A British government leaflet on Berlin a year after the building of the Wall stated: 'The Germans would regard it as a betrayal of the [Nato] alliance if Britain and the other western powers were to accept the division of Germany as permanent.' *The Meaning of Berlin*, HMSO, 1962.

46. Thatcher said she had already discussed the question with 'at least one other western leader' (meaning Mitterrand). Margaret Thatcher, *The Downing Street Years*, 1993, p.792.

47. Interview with *Der Spiegel*, Number 13, 1990, p.182.

48. Interview on the TV programme *Frost on Sunday*, 2.9.90.

49. Interview on BBC radio's Jimmy Young programme, 18.6.90. 'Your German population would go up to about 80 million and expand from there and it would be dominant both in numbers and in political and economic power.' Interviewer: 'And does that worry you?' Thatcher: 'Yes.'

50. Remarks to Karl-Günther von Hase at dinner, St Catharine's College, Cambridge, 30.3.90.

51. Interview with author in Bonn, 26.10.93. Thatcher was 'the only one who was honest.'

52. Thatcher, *op. cit.* p.747. She describes the atmosphere during the visit to the vineyard town of Deidesheim as 'Jolly, quaint, sentimental and slightly over-done. *Gemütlich* is, I think, the German word.'

53. The scene on 30.4.89 was witnessed by the author.

54. Powell: interview with author in London, 22.11.93.
55. British opposition to unity attracted still greater attention following an interview strongly critical of Germany in July 1990 by Nicholas Ridley, Britain's trade and industry secretary, who was subsequently forced to resign. There are, however, indications that the German government welcomed the opportunity given by such outbursts to reaffirm its reasoned approach to unification.
56. Memorandum on seminar at Chequers on 24.3.90. The document added: 'Two further aspects of the German character were cited as reasons for concern about the future. First, a capacity for excess, to overdo things, to kick over the traces. Second, a tendency to overestimate their own strengths and capabilities.' The memorandum was published in the *Independent on Sunday* and *Der Spiegel*.
57. Interview with author in London, 22.11.93.
58. Press conference in Bonn, 3.11.89.
59. Mitterrand's prediction was said to have taken place in a conversation with West German Chancellor Helmut Schmidt on 7.10.81. Mitterrand is quoted as saying the Soviet Union would collapse within fifteen years. Jacques Attali, *Verbatim*, 1993, p.107. Helmut Schmidt records a similar remark, but does not recollect Mitterrand giving any firm date. Schmidt, *Deutschland und seine Nachbarn*, 1990, p.256.
60. Powell described Mitterrand as 'really rattled' at an EC summit at Strasbourg in December 1990.
61. Thatcher is believed to have irritated Mitterrand by her description of his qualms over unification in her memoirs in 1993.
62. Attali, *Europe(s)*, 1994, p.42.
63. An internal report from the German embassy in Paris, leaked to the press in early January 1990, came to the conclusion that the French were 'playing for time' over the unification issue. *Frankfurter Allgemeine Zeitung*, 4.1.90. Horst Teltschik, Kohl's security adviser, confirming the *FAZ* report, wrote that the telegram was written by the German ambassador in Paris,

Franz Pfeffer. Teltschik described the publication of the document as 'irritating'. *329 Tage, Innenansichten der Einigung*, 1991, p.98.

64. Teltschik, *op. cit.* entries for 1.12.89 and 12.1.89, p.61 and 76.

65. Interview with author in Bonn, 26.10.93.

66. Kohl's private view was that Brian Mulroney, the Canadian prime minister, had also given German unity valuable support. Among European leaders, the chancellor cited Felipe González, the Spanish prime minister, as the only one to have provided wholehearted backing.

67. Walters' views on reunification were a surprise for ministers and officials in Bonn, as well as for US embassy staff. Among his interlocutors in Bonn, Kohl and Schäuble seem to have been least taken aback by his views. 'What happened was inevitable. It was less surprising to me than to the others.' Walters: interview with author in Bonn, 7.9.90.

68. Throughout the reunification saga, Walters seems to have benefited from Bush's support, but attracted increasing hostility from Baker. 'They [in Washington] could not forgive me for having so clearly foreseen the reunification of Germany.' Walters: *Die Vereinigung war Voraussehbar*, 1994, p. 64.

69. Although Baker's statements in favour of German unity may not always have been totally sincere, they were more elegantly formulated than remarks from the UK or France. At the opening of the talks on German unity in Bonn on 5.5.90, Baker pleased Genscher by alluding to the celebrated dictum of Thomas Mann. 'Rather than a German Europe . . . We want a European Germany.'

70. Author's private information.

71. Article in German foreign policy magazine *Aussenpolitik*, July 1994. Underscoring US understanding for Kohl's initial prevarications over the Polish border, Blackwill wrote: 'London and Paris took a much more critical line towards Kohl's position on borders and seemed to have more sympathy for the Polish view

than that of one of their closest friends and allies.'

72. Gorbachev, *Perestroika*, 1987, p.262.
73. Speech in the Kremlin, 24.10.93.
74. Thatcher, *op. cit.* p.792.
75. Speech in East Berlin, 6.10.89.
76. Mitterrand spoke after the meeting of the possibility that Gorbachev could be replaced by a Soviet general. Attali, *Verbatim*, 1993, p.43.
77. Kohl said Gorbachev was 'reflective' when he mentioned that unification might form a basis for a stable German–Soviet relationship. Interview with author in Bonn, 17.12.90.
78. Speech in Bonn, 9.11.90.
79. Kohl told the Bundestag on 15.2.90 that West Germany was bringing to the negotiating table with East Germany 'our strongest asset – the D-Mark.'
80. Expression used in February 1990.
81. Interview with *Die Welt*, 30.3.90.
82. Speech to the parliamentary council in Bonn, 8.5.49.
83. Dr Barbara Müller, in conversation with author in Dresden, 15.3.91.
84. Interview with author in Frankfurt an der Oder, 8.12.93.
85. Statement to Königswinter conference in Cambridge, 9.4.94.
86. In December 1993, according to an Allensbach poll, 57 per cent of East Germans believed socialism had been a 'good idea, which was carried out badly.' Only 24 per cent disagreed. In December 1993, 32 per cent termed democracy 'the best form for the state', but 30 per cent believed there was a 'better system'. *Frankfurter Allgemeine Zeitung*, 19.1.94.
87. According to police statistics, acts of violence perpetrated by right-wing extremists totalled 1,814 in 1993, against 2,584 in 1992. Eight people died in such incidents in 1993, against 17 in 1992.
88. An unusual example was a front-page editorial in the *Frankfurter Allgemeine Zeitung* on 23.6.92, containing the comment that the 'ghosts of Weimar' were coming again to the surface.

89. 'East Germany: Crime and Punishment', *New York Review of Books*, 14.5.92.

Chapter 3: A Difficult Transplant

1. *'Wirtschaftliche Probleme der Wiedervereinigung'*. Article in government press bulletin, 12.9.53.
2. Speech in the Bundestag, 10.5.90.
3. *Der Spiegel*, Number 39, 1991.
4. Conversation with author in Neu-Isenberg, 28.6.90.
5. Interview with *Die Welt*, 24.12.89.
6. Interview with *Der Spiegel*, Number 7, 1990.
7. Interview with *Süddeutsche Zeitung*, 2.6.90.
8. Speech in the Bundestag, 12.3.91.
9. *Sachverständigenrat*, 1993, p.210.
10. Federal spending for 1994, according to the 1993 projection, was DM478 billion. Waigel's 1990–94 budget plan, drawn up in early 1991, foresaw 1994 spending of DM421 billion.
11. Interview on German TV, 18.6.90.
12. Television address on 1.7.90.
13. Speech in Chemnitz, 20.4.94.
14. The Treuhand secured DM184 billion in investment guarantees, but it was also due to leave DM270 billion in debts, to be taken over by the state.
15. Figures taken from *Leistungsbilanz der Bundesregierung*, March 1994.
16. OECD report on Germany, July 1993, p.79.
17. OECD report on Germany, 1993. In the second half of 1990, East German earnings and productivity were 34.5 per cent and 29.5 per cent respectively of West German levels. In 1991, the figures were 47 per cent and 29 per cent; in 1992, 61.5 per cent and 35 per cent.
18. The measure of public sector borrowing includes funding by the federal railways, federal post office, the Treuhand and the East German housing authorities as well as that of the 'general government' – central, state and local government authorities and the social security system. After 1994, the government's budgetary accounts were

due to be reorganised, so that a single consolidated figure for the 'general government' would include all these borrowings with the exception of those of the federal post office.

19. The Maastricht treaty specified general government budget deficits of 3 per cent of GDP as one of the basic conditions for countries' participation in economic and monetary union, even though exceptions were permissible for member states that were reducing their deficits towards that level. In 1993, general government deficits of EC member states totalled more than 6 per cent. See Appendix II, p. 223.

20. *Sachverständigenrat*, 1993, p.113.

21. *Die Zeit*, 17.8.90.

22. Interview, *Wirtschaftswoche*, 2.3.90.

23. *Der Spiegel*, Number 2, 1994.

24. *Der Spiegel*, Number 39, 1991.

25. Jacques Rueff and André Piettre, *Wirtschaft ohne Wunder*, 1953.

26. Interview with author in London, 30.3.90.

27. Holger Schmieding, '*Die ostdeutsche Wirtschaftskrise: Ursachen und Lösungsstrategien*', Kiel Institute of World Economics, 1991.

28. Schmieding, *The End of the German Miracle? Germany's Prospects in Historical Perspective*, 1993.

29. Schmidt showed grudging admiration for Kohl's ability to seize the opportunity of unification, but he was otherwise a strong opponent of Kohl's policies. Schmidt himself was unprepared for the challenges. Before the fall of the Wall, he believed the 'German Question' would be solved only in the next century. *Die Zeit*, 13.9.89.

30. Schmidt, *Handeln für Deutschland*, 1993, p.26.

31. Speech to the Bundestag in Bonn, 28.11.89. Kohl irritated the US, France and the UK by communicating the contents of the speech to the German press before informing the three countries' ambassadors in Bonn. Horst Teltschik, who carried out both sets of briefings, apologised for this lapse on the grounds that the German newspapers needed to be told about the initiative

first because of their early deadlines. The speech was, however, remarkably anodyne by comparison with the unexpected flurry of action in ensuing months.

32. A group of US economists carried out an opinion poll among East German workers in 1990, which indicated that most East Germans would be willing to stay in the East in spite of low wages. 'The view that wages must be high is unfounded. Rather, the higher are wages, the greater is the price-cost squeeze, the more lay-offs there will be, and the fewer new jobs from investment; thus the higher will be unemployment. This unemployment will be the real cause of most out-migration.' University of California, Berkeley: 'East Germany In From The Cold: The Economic Aftermath of Currency Union', by George A. Akerlof *et al*, 18.4.91.

33. Interview with author in London, 30.3.90.

34. Interview with *Der Spiegel*, Number 7, 1990.

35. Speech in the Bundestag, Berlin, 4.10.90.

36. The idea was proposed in an article in *Die Zeit* on 19.1.90 by Ingrid Matthäus-Maier, deputy SPD floor-leader in the Bundestag. SPD press statement, 17.1.90.

37. *Münchner Merkur*, 20.1.90. Underlining his scepticism about the intrinsic value of the East Mark, Waigel, in January 1990, termed a D-Mark–East Mark rate of 1 to 5 rate as 'more realistic' than the 1 to 3 actually agreed to give East Germans access to D-Marks for short-term travel to the West.

38. Speech in Siegen, 25.1.90.

39. Special report by council of economic advisers, 20.1.90.

40. Interview with *Die Zeit*, 26.1.90.

41. Interview with author in Frankfurt, 29.1.90.

42. Teltschik has confirmed the importance of the 6 February meeting. 'On Monday [5 February] neither Kohl nor Waigel knew anything [about a plan for monetary union].' Interview with author in Gütersloh, 24.6.91.

43. Waigel lobbied against Pöhl both in 1979, when his Bundesbank appointment was decided, and in 1987 when it was renewed.

44. Finance Ministry statement, 2.2.90.

45. Author's private information. See also Theo Waigel, Manfred Schell, *Tage, die Deutschland und die Welt veränderten*, 1994, p. 17

46. The conversion of East Mark savings into D-Marks led to an increase of about 15 per cent in the German money supply, more than double the increase that would have been warranted by the relative size of the East German economy.

47. Interview with author in Bonn, 18.6.91.

48. Treaty on monetary, economic and social union, article 10. In October 1990, Detlev Rohwedder, the first president of the Treuhand agency, said East Germany might bring assets of DM600 billion into the unification process.

49. Interview with author in Bonn, 28.4.91.

50. '*Im Osten Deutschlands ein Mezzogiorno-Syndrom*', *Frankfurter Allgemeine Zeitung*, 13.1.93.

51. Interview with author in Munich, 24.9.93.

52. Estimate in spring 1990 by Günther Krause, who led the East German delegation during the monetary union negotiations.

53. press conference in Bonn, 9.2.90.

54. Speech in Kiel, 14.5.90. Ironically, Hesse's speech earned him criticism from Pöhl himself for its outspokenness.

55. DIW report, 8.2.90.

56. Interview with *Handelsblatt*, 19.2.90.

57. Five institutes' report, 8.4.90.

58. Forecast in July 1990.

59. *Handelsblatt*, 8.3.90.

60. Figure circulating within the European Commission in Brussels.

61. Hans-Jürgen Schmal, '*Sechs Thesen zur Währungsunion*', *Hamburger Abendblatt*, 20.2.90.

62. Dresdner Bank economic review, February 1990.

63. Speech at Dresdner Bank annual meeting, *Welt am Sonntag*, 1.7.90.

64. Sarrazin said difficulties in other countries such as southern Italy, Greece and Portugal were regarded, by contrast, as European problems. Remarks in Frankfurt, 14.9.93.

65. *Handelsblatt,* 27.2.90.
66. Scholey: Telephone conversation with author, 23.4.93.
67. Bundesbank annual report for 1992, p.30. *Sachverständigenrat,* 1993, p.128.
68. Article in the German trade union journal *Die Quelle,* January 1991 – *'Tarifpolitik: Die Einheitsquelle':* 'The eastern Reserve Army drives down western wages and threatens the unity of the unions. This is the reason for wanting a unified labour market as quickly as possible.'
69. West German managers and die-hard East German trade unionists were represented on the supervisory boards of the East German companies for which wage deals were concluded from 1990 onwards. Although inspired by differing motivations, they had similar interests in pushing through excessive wage awards.
70. The most important proposal for a wage subsidy scheme was made in the paper from the Akerlof group of economists quoted in Note 32.
71. Another idea for lowering East German production costs, put forward by Tyll Necker and Karl Schiller, was to exonerate East German companies from VAT payments. Kohl discussed this and several other ideas with Schiller, without apparently grasping the full import.
72. Underlining the effect of reduced East German export competitiveness on overall economic output, 'foreign demand' in the East German economy (including demand for East German goods from West Germany) fell 43 per cent in 1991.
73. In 1991, overall East German demand totalled DM352 billion, exceeding GDP by DM171 billion. In 1992, demand rose to DM431 billion, surpassing GDP by DM198 billion. In 1993, demand increased to DM484 billion, bringing the gap compared with GDP to DM206 billion.
74. The remaining 4 million (many of them women) either retired, stopped looking for work, crossed to the West or emigrated.
75. Gert Schmidt, economist at Industriekreditbank. Interview with author in Düsseldorf, January 1991.

76. Interview with author in Kronberg, 7.2.89.
77. A Social Democrat, Pöhl was termed by Kohl a member of the '*Schicki-Micki*' set – a 'champagne socialist'. Author's private information.
78. Lecture at the London School of Economics, 10.11.93.
79. '*Gesamtstaatliche Finanzpolitik in der Bewährung: Schuldenpolitische Aspekte der deutschen Einheit*', Walter Eucken Institut, 1991. Co-authored by Manfred Weber and Gerhard Ziebarth. The text states that the estimate for the 1994 debt figure includes incorporation of 'old debt' taken over from East Germany. When the paper was published in 1993 as the last chapter in a book co-authored by Schlesinger, Manfred Weber and Gerhard Ziebarth, the 1994 debt estimate was excised. Instead, the text spoke of public debt reaching DM2 trillion by the end of 1996. *Staatsverschuldung – ohne Ende? Zur Rationalität und Problematik des öffentlichen Kredits*, 1993.
80. Speech in Frankfurt, 11.6.91.
81. Interview with author in Bonn, 21.2.91.
82. *Trend* magazine, March 1990. Tietmeyer pointed out that access to reliable East German data was limited, and quoted an alternative (and more accurate) assessment by Wharton Economic Forecasting Associates that productivity levels in East Germany might be only 40 per cent of West Germany's.
83. Speech in Frankfurt, 10.3.94.
84. Interview with author in Bonn, 26.10.93.
85. Siegfried Schiller, from the Dresden-based Manfred-von-Ardenne Institute, forecast in an interview with *Handelsblatt* on 30.1.90 that the Comecon system would collapse.
86. Before unification, 70 per cent of East Germany's exports had been to the Comecon area, but the percentage plummeted in 1990–91.
87. Interview with author in Kronberg, 16.8.91.
88. The author is grateful to Brendan Brown for pointing out this lapse in the Bundesbank's policy response.
89. Speech in Potsdam, 13.11.91.

90. Speech in Zermatt, 8.8.93.
91. OECD report on Germany, July 1993, p. 10.
92. OECD report on West Germany, July 1990.
93. Horst Siebert, *Das Wagnis der Einheit*, 1993, p.76. The time needed for East Germany to increase per capita output to 80 per cent of the West German level is purely a matter of arithmetic. According to Siebert, if the growth rate difference between the two parts of Germany is 8 percentage points a year, then East Germany would need thirteen years (from 1991) to catch up. If the difference was 20 percentage points, then only five years would be required.
94. OECD report on Germany, July 1993, p. 29.

Chapter 4: Storm and Repair

1. Article in *Die Zeit*, March 1947, reprinted in *Im Wartesaal der Geschichte*, 1993.
2. Telephone conversation with author, October 1987.
3. Telephone interview with author, 2.3.94.
4. According to Erhard in 1954, 'That which has taken place in Germany these past six years was anything other than a miracle. It was merely the result of honest endeavour of a whole people, who again had the chance of applying human initiative, human liberty and human energies.' Speech in Paris, 7.12.54.
5. Speech in East Berlin, 15.2.81.
6. Article for the *Financial Times*, July 1990.
7. Between 1991 and 1993, an overall DM500 billion flowed into Germany from abroad – to banks and companies as well as the German public sector – through non-residents' purchases of securities and long-term credits. Fixed-interest securities purchases accounted for DM420 billion of this borrowing. Some of the bond market transactions were carried out by German citizens making their purchases via Luxembourg to avoid tax, but this does not change the overall picture of massive foreign borrowing. According to Bundesbank estimates, foreigners accounted for around DM438 billion of the public sector's

declared debt of DM1.44 trillion as of September 1993, compared with DM221 billion out of DM1.05 trillion debt at the end of 1990. Foreign borrowing by the public sector rose DM40 billion in the final quarter of 1993, taking overall foreign debt to around DM480 billion.

8. Net foreign assets fell during the 1990s as an inevitable consequence of Germany's move into current account deficit. According to Bundesbank statistics, net assets fell to DM435 billion in June 1993 from the peak of DM534 billion at the end of 1990.

9. Kohl was referring to the preamble in the 1949 West German constitution (*Grundgesetz*).

10. According to figures from the European statistics office (Eurostat), German GDP per capita in 1991, calculated on a common price basis (using purchasing power parity exchange rates) was Ecu15,858. The figure for West Germany (including Berlin) was Ecu18,401. This compared with an EC average of Ecu14,989, and a figure for the UK of Ecu14,732. While West Germany's GDP per capita was 23 per cent above the EC average, that of united Germany was only 6 per cent above the average.

11. Wallich, 'The "German Miracle" ', *The Yale Review*, 1955.

12. *Fortune* magazine's 1992 world ranking list, 26.7.93. This classification treats Royal Dutch/Shell and Unilever as fifty-fifty Anglo-Dutch companies. The German companies in the top sixty were Daimler-Benz, Volkswagen, Siemens, Hoechst, BASF, Bayer, Thyssen.

13. According to World Bank figures, based on GDP in constant 1987 dollar terms, West Germany in 1970 accounted for $852 billion of EC output of $2.9 trillion. In 1980, West Germany's GDP was $1.1 trillion out of EC GDP of $3.9 trillion. In 1993, united Germany accounted for GDP of $1.4 trillion out of EC GDP of $5 trillion.

14. These figures are based on constant dollar exchange rates. Using purchasing power parity exchange rates, the industrialised countries' share of world GDP is somewhat less.

15. H.G. Wells, *A Short History of the World*, 1922, (p.241 of revised 1946 Penguin edition).
16. Based on 1993 figures from Morgan Stanley, the US investment bank.
17. Report by Paolo Cecchini, EC Commission, 1988.
18. This expansion was well above West Germany's long-term potential for output growth, estimated by the Bundesbank at the end of the 1980s at a mere 2.5 per cent a year.
19. Regular EC surveys showed increasing disillusionment with the new arrangements among public opinion in EC countries. EC's Eurobarometer series.
20. Interview with author in Cologne, 14.3.89.
21. Necker returned to the Federation of German Industry (BDI) after his successor, Heinrich Weiss, fell out with top members of the organisation and failed to strike up a rapport with Chancellor Kohl.
22. Interview with author in Cologne, 15.1.93.
23. Interview with author in Bonn, 7.2.89.
24. Speech in Königswinter, 8.4.94.
25. Manufacturing as a share of GDP in West Germany declined from 38.4 per cent in 1970 to 31.2 per cent in 1989, at current prices, according to OECD figures. In the US, the share declined from 25.2 per cent in 1970 to 18.9 per cent in 1989; in the UK, from 28.7 per cent in 1970 to 18.9 per cent in 1988; in France, from 29.9 per cent to 21.0 per cent in 1990.
26. A landmark in the development of the German consensus system was the establishment after the national revolution in 1918 of a joint labour–employer body, the *Zentralarbeitsgemeinschaft*, to handle relations between the two sides of industry.
27. Quoted in Alan Watson, *The Germans: Who Are They Now?*, 1992, p.186.
28. According to Bundesbank figures, direct investment by foreign companies in Germany totalled DM565 million in 1993, against DM5.5 billion in 1992. Direct investment by German companies abroad totalled DM18.0 billion in 1993, against DM24.4 billion in 1992.

29. Interview with author in Düsseldorf, 13.9.94.
30. Necker invented the term 'DDR-II' for the economic system implanted in East Germany. *Frankfurter Allgemeine Zeitung*, 4.3.93.
31. John Craven, chairman of Morgan Grenfell, acquired by Deutsche Bank in 1989, who subsequently became a Deutsche Bank board member. Interview with author in London, 30.6.93.
32. Speech in Frankfurt, 22.12.88.
33. Interview with author in Frankfurt, 8.1.91.
34. Quoted in David Goodhart, *The Reshaping of the German Social Market*, 1994, pp. 17–18.
35. A report in January 1994 by Britain's Royal Society for the Encouragement of Arts, Manufactures and Commerce argued in favour of applying the 'stakeholder' approach to the UK.
36. Speech to the 100 Group of Finance Directors, London, 14.3.94.
37. David C. Roche, 'Restructuring and the Unbearable Process of European Disintegration', Morgan Stanley, 12.5.93.
38. Figures from *Sachverständigenrat*, 1993, and from Bundesbank publications.
39. OECD, *Economic Outlook*, December 1993. French costs, by comparison, showed a 3 per cent increase over 1991, and a 2 per cent fall compared with 1985. As a result, above all, of the weakening of the pound and the dollar over this time, British costs in 1993 were 20 per cent lower than in both years, while those in the US were 5 per cent below 1991 levels and 60 per cent below the position in 1985. In 1992, unit labour costs in West German manufacturing industry were 23 per cent higher than a weighted average of other industrial countries; in 1986, they had been 14 per cent lower than the international average. Institut der deutschen Wirtschaft, *IW-Trends*, Number 3, 1993. These figures exaggerate the loss of German competitiveness as they make no allowance for the differences in countries' economic cycles.

40. *Die Standortqualität der Bundesrepublik Deutschland,* 1992, Institut der deutschen Wirtschaft, March 1992.
41. Survey by the Association of German Chambers of Commerce, conducted with 8,500 industrial companies, 8.11.93. A total of 24 per cent had already carried out this step in the previous three years.
42. *Manufacturing Performance: A Scoreboard of Indicators for OECD Countries,* OECD, Paris, 1994.
43. *Ageing Populations,* OECD, 1988.
44. OECD, op. cit.
45. According to a projection at the end of 1993 by the Humboldt University in Berlin, East Germany's population could fall by about 25 per cent – nearly 4 million people – by 2010 as the result of a falling birthrate and migration, especially of twenty- to forty-year-olds.

Chapter 5: Fear of Drifting

1. In a letter to Lord Augustus Loftus, British ambassador to Berlin.
2. Interview with author in Bonn, 7.5.87.
3. 'Maastricht als historische Chance begreifen', *Frankfurter Allgemeine Zeitung,* 13.4.92.
4. *Frankfurter Allgemeine Zeitung,* 28.5.90.
5. 'The Community and German Unification', European Commission paper, 28.4.90.
6. *Financial Times,* 13.3.90.
7. The relaxation of trade restrictions was decided at the EC's Copenhagen summit in June 1993.
8. The European Commission has argued that there is 'no contradiction' between the principles of 'subsidiarity' and 'supranationality'. 'Some matters are best decided at the level of the European Community or the Union, others should be left to national governments or may best be dealt with at the level of regional or local government.' 'European Union: The Ways and the Means', European Commission, 2.4.92.
9. The most celebrated previous Community plan for Emu, formulated in 1970 by a committee under Pierre Werner,

the Luxembourg prime minister, proposed that budgetary policy should be decided at a Community level.

10. The Bundesbank repeatedly stressed that a monetary union required 'a comprehensive political union if it is to prove durable.' Statements by Bundesbank council, September 1990 and February 1992.

11. Elisabeth Noelle-Neumann, in telephone conversation with author, 21.4.94.

12. See, for instance, Gerd Langguth, *'Die Einstellung der Deutschen zu Europa', Die Sonde*, Numbers 1 and 2, 1989.

13. Jean-François Revel, former editor of French magazine *L'Express, 'Die unnötige Furcht vor den Deutschen', Frankfurter Allgemeine Zeitung*, 9.6.90.

14. Interview with author in Bonn, 7.2.89. Rather than *Wiedervereinigung*, Kohl said he preferred the phrase *Einheit der Nation* (unity of the nation). 'Under *Wiedervereinigung* one understood something else, the attachment of the GDR [East Germany] to the Federal Republic . . . The idea – the vision – is that we want the political unity of Europe.'

15. Because East Germany had been recognised as a separate state, but not as a foreign country, Bonn's relations towards East Germany were formally separated from foreign policy.

16. Speech in Berlin 13.3.91.

17. According to a French Finance Ministry report, 'The first paradox of unification is that it will result in the first instance in a weakening of the German economy . . . Once these problems are surmounted, at the end of the century Germany will be – even more than today – the dominant economic power in Europe.' Alain Boublil, *'Les Consequences Economiques de l'Unification de l'Allemagne'*, 20.11.90.

18. Speech to the United Nations general assembly, 26.9.90.

19. Interview in *Süddeutsche Zeitung*, 19.5.92.

20. Interview with author in London, 5.11.93.

21. Interview in *Le Monde*, 19.4.94.

22. CDU/CSU paper on European integration, 1.9.94.

23. Schmidt, *Handeln für Deutschland*, 1993, p.134.

24. Interview with author in Hamburg, 16.4.93.
25. In 1992, Germany's exports to central and eastern Europe (including the former Soviet Union) were DM37 billion, compared with DM40 billion to Austria. Exports to France (DM87 billion) were six times greater than to the former Soviet Union (DM13 billion).
26. Conversation with author in Frankfurt, 15.5.90.
27. According to Hans-Dietrich Genscher, the German foreign minister, united Germany would have 'a higher political and economic weight . . . We do not want to turn this into a search for more power, rather for more responsibility.' Interview with author in Bonn, 14.9.90. By contrast, Pierre Bérégovoy, French finance minister and later prime minister, spoke of his wartime experiences: 'I am one of those who experienced the effects of the great German Reich.' French TV, 15.10.89.
28. *'Nous devons veiller à ce ne se crée pas un déséquilibre qui finalement s'achéverait dans une sorte de reconstitution de l'Europe des guerres. Non pas que je prédise une guerre, mais nous risquerions de retrouver la situation de l'Europe qui s'est précipités avant 1914 dans un statut qui a abouti à une situation explosive et des drames immenses.'* Press conference in East Berlin, 22.12.89.
29. Speech to the Bundesrat, Bonn, 22.12.89.
30. At the initiative of Balladur and French prime minister Jacques Chirac, a Franco-German monetary council was set up in 1987 to try to bring French influence to bear on the Bundesbank's policies. The council lapsed into disuse in the 1990s.
31. *'Il faut repenser l'Europe'*, *Le Monde*, 16.11.89.
32. Speech in Munich, 17.9.90.
33. The 1970 Werner Plan had called for monetary union by 1980, but was dropped after the Bretton Woods system collapsed in 1973.
34. Interview with author in London, 1.4.93.
35. Remarks at dinner in Paris, 14.4.94.
36. Interview with *La Croix*, 26.8.93.
37. The Delors committee was set up by the EC summit in Hanover in June 1988. Composed largely of central

bankers, it stressed the importance of economic convergence as a condition for Emu.

38. A discussion paper by Genscher, in February 1987, in favour of monetary union had given early impetus to the idea.

39. As one Commission official wrote, 'The near-unanimous view that German unification implied a need to accelerate European union was a heaven-sent opportunity to focus minds on preparatory talks and to settle a starting date for negotiations.' David Spence, *Enlargement without Accession: The EC's Response to German Unification*, Royal Institute of International Affairs, 1991.

40. Powell: interview with author in London, 22.11.93.

41. EC communiqué at Strasbourg summit, 9.12.91.

42. Joint message to other EC leaders, 19.4.90.

43. The statement appeared to mean that a treaty providing for economic and monetary union could come into effect by 1 January 1993.

44. Speech in the Bundestag, 28.4.90.

45. Speech in Frankfurt, 11.6.91.

46. Interview with author in Rome, 5.4.93. Andreotti's scepticism about German unity had been manifested in 1984: 'There exist two German states and there should remain two German states.'

47. Budget deficits had to be limited to 3 per cent of GDP, while public sector debt had to be limited to 60 per cent of GDP. Exceptions were allowable if a country's deficit was deemed 'exceptional and temporary' or if debt was approaching the 60 per cent figure 'at a satisfactory pace'. Countries eligible for Emu had also to maintain inflation and interest rates within 1.5 and 2 percentage points respectively of the three best performing EC states. Further, qualifying countries would have to keep their currencies stable within the EMS during the previous two years.

48. The results of the Maastricht conference did not, however, match up to Kohl's original hopes of winning concrete concessions from his partners on full-scale political union. In the days before the Maastricht meeting,

Kohl had declared, 'Political union and economic and monetary union are inseparably linked . . . We cannot and will not give up sovereignty over monetary policies if political union remains a castle in the air.' Speech in Jouy-en-Josas, 3.12.91.

49. Interview with author in Paris 28.4.92. Balladur predicted that, although the monetary union provisions of the Maastricht treaty had been dubbed 'irreversible', national parliaments would have the final say, 'I don't think things will happen in the way described by the treaty.'

50. See also Jack Lang, culture minister and confidant of Mitterrand: 'There is deep admiration for Germany. But also a certain anxiety. If Europe's development runs into problems, Germany could strike out on its own and seek new alliances.' Interview with *Der Spiegel*, Number 36, 1992.

51. Article in *Le Monde*, 21.8.92.

52. Opinion poll by BVA survey organisation, *Libération*, 22.9.92.

53. Before the Maastricht conference, German newspapers largely ignored the Emu question. When the summit took place, headlines attacking the plan suddenly appeared in *Bild-Zeitung*, Germany's most popular daily newspaper, and *Der Spiegel*, the bestselling news magazine.

54. Interview with *Süddeutsche Zeitung*, 11.10.90.

55. When citing this call for European unification by Winston Churchill (speech in Zurich, 19.9.46), Kohl appeared not to recognise that, according to Churchill, Britain would remain outside any 'United States of Europe'. 'In this urgent work, France and Germany must take the lead together. Great Britain, the British Commonwealth of Nations, mighty America – and, I trust, Soviet Russia, for then indeed all would be well – must be the friends and sponsors of the new Europe and must champion its right to live.'

56. Speech in Washington, 20.5.91.

57. Dietrich von Kyaw, at Maastricht, 9.12.91.

58. The EC agreed in October 1993 that the European Monetary Institute, the European central bank's forerunner, should be set up in Frankfurt.

59. *'Deutschland ohne DM?' Der Spiegel*, Number 50, 1991. The magazine's cover story for the weekend in which the Maastricht conference took place was entitled *'Angst um die D-Mark'*.

60. Interview with *Europa* magazine, December 1991.

61. In December 1991, according to the Allensbach Institute, only 10 per cent of West Germans and 11 per cent of East Germans favoured accelerating moves towards a 'united Europe', compared with 19 per cent in March 1990, 28 per cent in March 1989, 34 per cent in September 1988 and 51 per cent in January 1988 and 60 per cent in March 1984 (latter figures for West Germany only). *Frankfurter Allgemeine Zeitung*, 15.1.92.

62. Allensbach poll, *Frankfurter Allgemeine Zeitung*, 23.6.92.

63. Mannheimer Forschungsgruppe Wahlen, *Süddeutsche Zeitung*, 18.9.92.

64. Elisabeth Noelle-Neumann, *'Gegen einen Bundestaat Europa'*, 1992.

65. Kohl explained that the expression was used as their equivalent of the United States of America. Speech in Vienna, 18.5.93.

66. The chief surprise about German opposition to monetary union is that it did not surface earlier. Karl Otto Pöhl, Bundesbank president, pointed out in 1989, 'If the idea spread and the German population understood what it [European Monetary Union] is about – namely, that it centres on their money, and that decisions on it would be taken not by the Bundesbank, but by a new institution – then I would imagine that considerable resistance might arise.' Interview with author in Frankfurt, 29.6.89.

67. Augstein's commentaries in 1991–92, in the aftermath of the Maastricht treaty, earned him hostility in Paris. See interview with Augstein in *Le Figaro*, 25.8.93.

68. The anti-Maastricht party founded by Manfred Brunner, a former top Brussels civil servant who quit his job over

opposition to the treaty, was an attempt to combine anti-Maastricht sentiment with a liberal economic and political position.

69. Bundesbank monthly report, November 1993.
70. Interview with *Süddeutsche Zeitung*, 2.11.93.
71. Statement by sixty economists led by Professor Renate Ohr (Hohenheim) and Professor Wolf Schäfer (Hamburg), *'Wirtschaftswissenschaftler zu den Beschlüssen von Maastricht'*, June 1992.
72. Speech to the Bundestag, 13.12.91.
73. Statement by the Federal Constitutional Court, 12.10.93.
74. Bonn government statement, 12.10.93.
75. According to the Constitutional Court, the Bundestag and Bundesrat would be able to give a legally binding judgement on which countries were deemed to fulfil the arithmetical 'convergence criteria' governing their suitability for inclusion in Emu. In 1991, Waigel had told other EC finance ministers that there would be 'scope for political judgement' in deciding which countries were allowed to go through to 'stage three'. However, this scope seems likely to be virtually non-existent.
76. Even though this two-year rule would not apply until 1995 – two years ahead of the earliest possible date for Emu of 1997 – it created an extra hurdle, preventing countries from making timely exchange rate adjustments.
77. Bonn's large interest rate subsidies to support East German capital investment had the additional effect of increasing the cost of credit for non-German borrowers. Because of the distortions caused by these subsidies, the Bundesbank had to raise German interest rates to higher levels than would otherwise have been necessary to slow down German credit creation. This intensified the pain for borrowers outside Germany without access to subsidised loans.
78. In confidential discussions in spring 1990, the Bundesbank tried to launch a broad ERM realignment, but it received a general rebuff. Talks were held with the

Bank of Italy as well as with the French and Dutch
authorities. The Bundesbank again broached the idea
in 1991, but no formal application to change parities
was made by the Bonn government. France, in particular, was opposed to any change of the franc's parity
against the D-Mark. It is worth noting, however, that
the International Monetary Fund was in favour of a
D-Mark revaluation. For a considered view at the time
by IMF economists, see Leslie Lipschitz & Donogh
McDonald, *German Unification: Economic Issues*, 1990,
p. 103.

79. Thatcher was persuaded to approve ERM entry by
being promised that it could be combined with a one
percentage point cut in interest rates, announced on
5 October. The Treasury decision to cut rates before
Britain entered the ERM came in spite of a letter
of protest to Thatcher from Bank of England governor Leigh-Pemberton, who wrote, 'I implore you not
to take the dividend [of lower interest rates] before
it is earned.' Unpublished Bank of England letter,
5.10.90.

80. Karl Otto Pöhl: conversation with author in Frankfurt,
9.6.93. The existence of the telephone call is confirmed
by the British Treasury, although there is no record on
the Treasury files of Pöhl's comments during the conversation.

81. Leigh-Pemberton, in conversation with the author in
London, 23.11.93, confirmed that he was unaware of
the telephone call. Eddie George, the deputy governor
of the Bank of England, who took over as governor in
1993, was, however, aware of it. Normally, communications with the Bundesbank were a matter for the Bank,
not the Treasury.

82. The Bath meeting, at which Lamont nearly caused
Schlesinger to walk out after four times asking him to
cut interest rates, was spectacularly unsuccessful. The
German and Dutch delegations were ready to discuss a
currency realignment, and Schlesinger made a vaguely
worded suggestion in this direction. But no one at the

meeting paid it any attention, primarily because the French government did not want to upset the currency markets in advance of the French referendum on the Maastricht treaty on 20 September.

83. On 15.9.92, Schlesinger hinted in a newspaper interview that a realignment, already decided at the weekend of 12–13 September for the Italian lira, might have to be extended to other currencies. The remarks, when communicated to news agencies that evening, triggered a sharp run on the sterling exchange rate. In briefings with journalists on the evening of 15.9.92, Downing Street officials criticised Schlesinger and other Bundesbank officials for contributing to pressure on sterling.

84. Interview on BBC radio, 18.9.92.

85. See for instance Lamont's interview with the *Financial Times*, 31.12.91.

86. Conversation with author in London, 16.12.93.

87. Otto Schlecht: telephone conversation with author, 21.9.93.

88. Conversation with author in Frankfurt, 3.12.93.

89. Interview with author in Copenhagen, 29.3.93.

90. Speech in Frankfurt, 21.1.94.

91. Speech in Frankfurt, 25.3.94.

92. Speech in Bonn, 25.1.94. Professor Uwe Jens, the Social Democratic Party's (SPD) economic affairs spokesman, recommended that the monetary union target date of 1997 or 1999 should be postponed for ten years. Press conference in London, 28.1.94. Oskar Lafontaine, the SPD's shadow finance minister, claimed just before the October 1994 elections that, if elected, the SPD would renegotiate the terms of the plan for economic and monetary union (Emu) to guarantee monetary stability.

93. For instance, Genscher, in an article for the *Financial Times*, 16.5.92: Maastricht is 'a forward looking strategy by which both enlargement and deepening will be pursued as a parallel process.'

94. For instance, Kohl in address broadcast by radio and TV, 31.12.89: 'We must strive together for German unity and European unity. Germany is our Fatherland,

Europe our future! The European Community must not
end at the Elbe.'

95. For instance, Waigel in interview with *Welt am Sonntag*,
24.12.89: 'Herr Minister: What is more important? Stable
money or common European money?' Waigel: 'Common,
stable money in Europe.'

96. Germany's determination in March 1994 to press for EC
accession by Sweden, Austria, Finland and Norway provoked a diplomatic tussle with France. Germany made
widening membership to central and eastern Europe a
priority during its six-monthly EC presidency in the second half of 1994.

97. The additional costs would arise from the transfer to
the East of massive sums in agricultural subsidies and
cash for poorer regions under the Common Agricultural Policy and the EC's Structural Funds. According to
Professor Richard Baldwin of the Graduate Institute of
International Studies in Geneva, bringing in the Czech
republic, Hungary, Poland and Slovakia by 1999 would
increase the EC's budget that year by an overall Ecu58
billion (74 per cent) from the projected levels for that
year of Ecu86 billion on the basis of unchanged EC
policies. Baldwin, *Towards An Integrated Europe*, 1994.

98. Kohl was more interested in setting a process in train
than establishing timetables, and damped speculation
that eastern European countries could rapidly become
full EC members. Press conference in London, 27.4.94.

Chapter 6: Germany in the Europe to Come

1. Speech at conference on Germany in Berlin, 25.1.54.
2. Press conference in Paris, 4.2.65.
3. Speech in Prague to welcome President Richard von
Weizsäcker, 15.2.90.
4. *New York Times*, 7.1.90.
5. Speech to the United Nations, 26.9.90: 'For all time
the principles enshrined in our constitution – human
rights and human dignity, democracy and the rule of
law, social justice and respect for creation, peace and

good-neighbourly relations – will govern our thoughts and actions.'

6. Heine, '*Deutschland: Ein Wintermärchen*', 1844.
7. *Frankfurter Allgemeine Zeitung*, 31.12.93.
8. The author records his debt to Michael Stürmer (speech in Munich, 21.5.93) for the comparison between the Maastricht treaty and Bismarck's celebrated watch.

Bibliography

In view of the large number of books on contemporary and historical German and European issues, this list is limited to those to which reference has been made in the text, or which bear specific relevance to its subject matter.

Politics/General

Attali, Jacques, *Europe(s)*, Paris, 1994.

Attali, Jacques, *Verbatim*, Paris, 1993.

Bahr, *Zum europäischen Frieden*, Berlin, 1988.

Balfour, Michael, *Germany: The Tides of Power*, London/New York, 1992.

Brandt, Willy, *Erinnerungen*, Berlin, 1989.

Calleo, David, *The German Problem Reconsidered*, Cambridge, 1978

Childs, Brian, *Germany since 1918*, London, 1971 (2nd edition, 1980).

Cole, Alistair, *François Mitterrand*, London, 1994.

Dahrendorf, Ralf, *Gesellschaft und Demokratie in Deutschland*, Munich, 1965.

Dennis, Mike, *German Democratic Republic: Politics, Economics and Society*, London, 1988.

Bibliography

Dönhoff, Marion Gräfin, *Im Wartesaal der Geschichte*, Stuttgart, 1993.

Garton Ash, Timothy, *In Europe's Name*, London, 1993.

Geipel, Gary L. (ed.), *Germany in a New Era*, Indianapolis, 1993.

Goodhart, David, *The Reshaping of the German Social Market*, London, 1994.

Grosser, Alfred, *Mein Deutschland*, Hamburg, 1993.

Herles, Wolfgang, *Geteilte Freude*, Munich, 1992.

Herzberg, Andert, *Der Sturz: Honecker im Kreuzverhör*, Berlin, 1991.

James, Harold & Stone, Marla (eds.), *When the Wall Came Down*, London/New York, 1992.

Kohl, Helmut, *Bilanzen und Perspektiven: Regierungspolitik 1989–91* (2 volumes), Bonn, 1992.

von Krockow, Christian Graf, *Die Deutschen vor ihrer Zukunft*, Berlin, 1993.

Leif, Thomas, Legrand, Hans-Josef & Klein, Ansgar (eds.), *Die Politische Klasse in Deutschland*, Bonn/Berlin, 1992.

Padgett, Stephen (ed.), *Parties and Party Systems in the New Germany*, Aldershot, 1993.

Pond, Elizabeth, *Beyond the Wall: Germany's Road to Unification*, New York, 1993.

Sauzay, Brigitte, *Die rätselhaften Deutschen*, Stuttgart, 1986.

Schmidt, Helmut, *Die Deutschen und ihre Nachbarn*, Berlin, 1990.

Schmidt, Helmut, *Handeln für Deutschland*, Hamburg, 1993.

Stürmer, Michael, *Die Grenzen der Macht*, Berlin, 1992.

Thatcher, Margaret, *The Downing Street Years*, London, 1993.

Teltschik, Horst, *329 Tage, Innenansichten der Einigung*, Berlin, 1991.

Watson, Alan, *The Germans: Who Are They Now?*, London, 1992.

Walters, Vernon, *Die Vereinigung war voraussehbar*, Berlin, 1994.

Whitney, Craig, *Advocatus Diaboli: Wolfgang Vogel, Anwalt zwischen Ost und West*, Berlin, 1993.

Economics

Erhard, Ludwig, *Wohlstand für Alle*, Düsseldorf, 1957.

Erhard, Ludwig, *Deutsche Wirtschaftspolitik*, Düsseldorf, 1962.

Henzler, Herbert A. & Späth, Lothar, *Sind die Deutschen noch zu retten?*, Munich, 1993.

Hickel, Rudolf & Priewe, Jan, *Nach dem Fehlstart*, Frankfurt, 1994.

Lipschitz, Leslie & McDonald, Donogh)eds.), *German Unification: Economic Issues*, Washington, 1990.

Nölling, Wilhelm, *Unser Geld*, Berlin/Frankfurt, 1993.

Ogger, Günter, *Nieten in Nadelstreifen*, Munich, 1992.

Organisation for Economic Cooperation and Development, *Annual Report on Germany*, Paris, 1993.

Rueff, Jacques & Piettre, André, *Wirtschaft ohne Wunder*, Erlenbach/Zurich, 1953.

Sachverständigenrat, *Jahresgutachten 1993–94*, Stuttgart, 1993.

Schiller, Karl, *Der schwierige Weg in die offene Gesellschaft*, Berlin, 1994.

Schlesinger, Helmut, Weber, Manfred & Ziebarth, Gerhard, *Staatsverschuldung – Ohne Ende?*, Darmstadt, 1993.

Schmieding, Holger, *The End of the German Mira-*

cle?: Germany's Prospects in Historical Perspective, London, 1993

Siebert, Horst, *Das Wagnis der Einheit*, Stuttgart, 1993.

Siebert, Horst, *Geht den Deutschen die Arbeit aus?*, Munich, 1994.

Sinn, Gerlide & Sinn, Hans-Werner, *Jumpstart: The Economic Unification of Germany*, London, 1992.

Smyser, W.R., *The Economy of United Germany*, New York, 1992.

Waigel, Theo & Schell, Manfred, *Tage, die Deutschland und die Weltveränderten*, Munich, 1994.

Wallich, Henry, *Mainsprings of the German Revival*, New Haven, 1955.

Wehner, Burkhard, *Deutschland stagniert*, Darmstadt, 1994.

Europe

Baldwin, Richard, *Towards An Integrated Europe*, London, 1994.

Buchan, David, *Europe: The Strange Superpower*, Aldershot, 1993.

Driffill, John & Beber, Massimo (eds), *A Currency for Europe*, London, 1991.

Duff, Andrew (ed.), *Subsidiarity within the European Community*, London, 1993.

Flemming, John & Rollo, Jim, *Trade, Payments and Adjustment in Central and Eastern Europe*, London, 1992.

Grant, Charles, *Delors: Inside the House that Jacques Built*, London, 1994.

Krause, Axel, *Inside the New Europe*, New York, 1991.

Schmieding, Holger, *Europe after Maastricht*, London, 1993.

Simonian, Haig, *The Privileged Partnership: Franco-German Relations in the European Community*, Oxford, 1985.

Spence, David, *Enlargement Without Accession: The EC's Response To German Unification*, London, 1991.

Temperton, Paul (ed.), *The European Currency Crisis*, Cambridge/Chicago, 1993.

Tsoukalis, Loukas, *The New European Economy*, Oxford, 1993.

Weber, Manfred (ed.), *Europa auf dem Weg zur Währungsunion*, Darmstadt, 1991.

Appendices

I. EC political leaders

from the fall of the Berlin Wall to the aftermath of Maastricht (prime minister except where stated)

Belgium	Wilfried Martens (Christian People's Party) 1981–92 Jean-Luc Dehaene (Christian People's Party) 1992–
Denmark	Poul Schlüter (Conservative People's Party) 1982–93 Poul Nyrup Rasmussen (Social Democratic Party) 1993–
France	François Mitterrand* (Socialist Party) 1981– Michel Rocard (Socialist Party) 1988–91 Edith Cresson (Socialist Party) 1991–92 Pierre Bérégovoy (Socialist Party) 1992–93 Edouard Balladur (Rally for the Republic) 1993–
Germany†	Helmut Kohl** (Christian Democratic Union) 1982–
Greece	Constantine Mitsotakis (New Democracy) 1989–93 Andreas Papandreou (Panhellenic Socialist Movement) 1981–89, 1993–

* president ** chancellor † before 1990, West Germany only

Ireland	Charles Haughey (Fiana Fail) 1987–92 Albert Reynolds (Fiana Fail) 1992–
Italy	Luigi Ciriaco De Mita (Christian Democratic Party) 1988–89 Giulio Andreotti (Christian Democratic Party) 1989–92 Giuliano Amato (Socialist Party) 1992–93 Carlo Azeglio Ciampi (non-party) 1993–94 Silvio Berlusconi (Forza Italia) 1994–
Luxembourg	Jacques Santer (Christian Social Party) 1984–94
Netherlands	Ruud Lubbers (Christian Democratic Party) 1982–94 Wim Kok (Labour Party) 1994–
Spain	Felipe González (Socialist Party) 1982–
Portugal	Anibal Cavaco Silva (Social Democratic Party) 1985–
UK	Margaret Thatcher (Conservative Party) 1979–90 John Major (Conservative Party) 1990–
EC Commission	Jacques Delors (president) 1985–1994 Jacques Santer (president) 1995–

II. International economic performance

Annual changes in real gross domestic product

	Germany	France	Italy	UK	US	Industrial countries
1989	3.6	4.3	2.9	2.1	2.5	3.3
1990	5.7	2.5	2.1	0.4	1.2	2.4
1991	1.0	0.7	1.2	−2.2	−0.7	0.6
1992	2.1	1.4	0.7	−0.6	2.6	1.6
1993	−1.2	−0.7	−0.7	1.9	3.0	1.2
1994*	1.8	1.8	1.5	2.8	4.0	2.6

* projections. Up to 1990, West Germany only.
Source: International Monetary Fund, OECD

III. The EC and the Maastricht convergence criteria (1993)

		Inflation %	Budget deficit % of GDP	Interest rate %	Govt. debt % of GDP	EMS position	Ready for Emu?
Target		3.1	3.0	9.5	60.0		
France	(3)	2.1*	5.9	6.8*	44.9*	Wide Band	No
Germany	(3)	4.2	3.3	6.5*	48.9*	Narrow Band*	No
Ireland	(3)	1.4*	3.0*	7.7*	92.9	Wide Band	No
Luxmbrg	(3)	3.6	2.5*	6.9*	10.0*	Wide Band	No
Nethrlnd	(3)	2.1*	4.0	6.3*	83.1	Narrow band*	No
UK	(3)	1.6*	7.6	7.5*	53.2*	Floating	No
Belgium	(2)	2.8*	7.4	7.2*	138.4	Wide Band	No
Denmark	(2)	1.3*	4.4	7.2*	78.5	Wide Band	No
Spain	(1)	4.6	7.2	10.2	55.6*	Wide Band	No
Greece	(0)	14.4	15.4	21.2	113.6	Floating**	No
Italy	(0)	4.5	10.0	11.4	115.8	Floating	No
Portugal	(0)	6.5	8.9	12.5	69.5	Wide Band	No

1993 figures

Source: European Commission, national statistics

Figures in brackets indicate number of five criteria met in 1993.

Wide Band refers to 15 per cent fluctuation margins established on 2 August 1993.

Narrow Band (for Germany and Netherlands only) refers to 2.25 per cent fluctuation band preserved for D-Mark/guilder link.

* Maastricht targets achieved
**Managed drachma float against D-Mark

The five criteria for membership of Emu in 1997 or 1999:
1. Annual change in consumer prices should not be more than 1.5 points above three lowest EC inflation rates.
2. General government budget deficits must not be more than 3 per cent of gross domestic product, apart from in exceptional circumstances.
3. Yields of long-term government bonds should not exceed yields of the three lowest-inflation countries by more than 2 percentage points.

4. General government debt should not exceed 60 per cent of GDP.
5. Currencies should be in 'normal' EMS bands for two years prior to final fixing of exchange rates.

IV. The German Bundestag election (1994)

The German Bundestag election on 16 October was the second since Germany was unified in 1990 and the thirteenth since the establishment of the Federal Republic of Germany in 1949. The centre-right coalition under Chancellor Helmut Kohl, in office in Bonn since 1982, was confirmed in power. The Bundestag majority of the coalition, consisting of the Christian Democratic Union, Christian Social Union and Free Democratic Party, fell from 134 to 10 seats.

The election results were as follows (number of seats in brackets):

	October 1994	December 1990
Christian Democratic Union & Christian Social Union	41.5% (294)	43.8% (319)
Free Democratic Party	6.9% (47)	11.0% (79)
Social Democratic Party	36.4% (252)	33.5% (239)
Alliance 90/Greens	7.3% (49)	3.8% (8)
Party of Democratic Socialism (former East German communist party)	4.4% (30)	2.4% (17)
Republicans	1.9%	2.1%
Turnout	79.1%	77.8%

● Triumph for Kohl

Despite the sharp fall in the ruling coalition's majority, the result was a personal triumph for Kohl, who had been trailing in the opinion polls at the beginning of 1994. Kohl owed his victory above all to a more buoyant than expected economic recovery in West and East Germany since spring 1994. Even though German voters' incomes were continuing to fall in real terms because of tax rises and low nominal wage increases, rising economic confidence – as often the case in Germany – favoured the incumbent government. Other factors contributing to the Chancellor's success were his own personal authority, campaigning mistakes by his Social Democratic challenger, Rudolf Scharping (in particular, clumsy handling of SPD plans to raise taxes) and the natural conservatism of the German electorate, which has never voted a government out of office in the post-war period.

One of the main points of controversy in the campaign centred on whether, in the event of a 'hung' parliament, the SPD would seek to form a government with the aid of the reformed East German communists, the Party of Democratic Socialism. The SPD made a tactical error by forming a minority government 'tolerated' by the PDS earlier in 1994 in the East German state of Saxony-Anhalt, allowing the CDU/CSU to claim that the SPD would carry out a similar move to gain power in Bonn. In view of visceral anti-communism among the West German electorate – particularly among older voters (the over-60s make up more than a quarter of the electorate) – this proved to be an effective electoral strategem by the CDU/CSU.

- **Still a divided Germany**

The most striking feature of the election was the difference in voting patterns and behaviour between East and West Germany. In December 1990, when post-unification euphoria was still strong, the CDU/CSU and FDP performed equally well in both parts of the country. After the economic difficulties and high unemployment of the past four years, in 1994 the coalition parties scored only 42 per cent of the vote in East Germany against nearly 50 per cent in the West. In the East, voting participation fell 1.8 percentage points compared with the 1990 election, while it rose 2.2 points in the West.

Saxony, traditionally the economically strongest region of East Germany, was the only East German state to show a majority for the governing coalition. In all other states, the left-wing parties – SPD, PDS and Greens – were out in front. However, splitting of the left-wing vote between the SPD and PDS (which gained 20 per cent of overall East German votes, finishing in third place behind the CDU and SPD) deprived the SPD of a large part of its potential strength in East Germany. The widespread desire to elect the PDS as the representative of East Germans' interests underlined how the differences in political culture between East and West Germany have become more marked since unification.

● **Questions for coalition**

The election did not produce only positive points for Kohl:

– It showed an unusual degree of political fragmentation. The three mainstream groupings – CDU/CSU, FDP and SPD – recorded their lowest combined score since 1953.

– German voters showed signs of fatigue after an intensive series of state, local and European elections in 1994. Turnout was 79.1 per cent, up from 77.8 per cent in 1990, but was the third lowest since the war.

– The Party of Democratic Socialism (PDS), Kohl's chief adversary during the election campaign, gained parliamentary representation and doubled its share of the vote compared with 1990. Although the PDS fell below the 5 per cent threshold, it won seats in parliament by fulfilling the condition of gaining more than three parliamentary mandates outright (under the first of the two votes cast in the German electoral system).

– The CDU/CSU score, at 41.5 per cent, was 2.3 percentage points lower than in 1990, and the lowest since 1949 (when it was an unusually low 31 per cent). It compares with an average for the previous eleven elections (not counting the unusual circumstances of the 1949 poll) of 46.3 per cent.

– The CDU/CSU's coalition partner, the Free Democratic Party, maintained its place in the Bundestag after exceeding the 5 per cent voting threshold needed for parliamentary representation. However, the FDP's score was the second lowest since 1949 (only in 1969 did it fare worse). After a series of defeats in Land elections, there is still a question mark over the FDP's long-term future.

– The coalition's overall score (48.4 per cent) marked a fall of 7.4 percentage points from its share of the vote in Kohl's first successful general election in 1983.

– The SPD score of 36.4 per cent was up 2.9 points from 1990. Although this was well below the average of the previous eleven elections of 38.1%, the SPD managed to reverse a run of three successive elections of lower scores (1983, 1987, 1990).

● **Kohl's position**

Despite the narrowness of his victory margin, Kohl's dominance of German politics was confirmed. He became only the second post-war German chancellor to win four successive elections. (West Germany's first chancellor, Konrad Adenauer, was victorious in 1949, 1953, 1957 and 1961). If he remains in office until half-way through the four year legislative period, Kohl will exceed Adenauer's record fourteen years in office. Kohl's importance on the European stage has been amplified by the departure of most of the leaders who agreed the Maastricht treaty in December 1991. Following the departure of President François Mitterrand, only four of the twelve leaders who gave their blessing to the treaty are still in office. This has magnified the Chancellor's role in discussions about the next stage of European integration.

After the election, Kohl denied that the coalition would be unstable, pointing out that his predecessors Willy Brandt (in 1972) and Helmut Schmidt (in 1976) ruled throughout a legislative term with similarly slender majorities. Kohl had some important arguments on his side. Unlike Britain, Germany does not have by-elections during a legislative period. If a parliamentary deputy dies or resigns, he or she is automatically replaced by another candidate from the party list.

In the past in West Germany, changes of chancellor have come about (in 1969 and 1982) through the Free Democrats prompting a switch in coalition allegiances. The FDP is clearly the weak link in the CDU-led government. However, its poor election showing lowers the likelihood that the FDP will desert the CDU/CSU in mid-term and join the SPD. By 1994, the party became progressively viewed as a form of ersatz Christian Democrat party, and lost some of the commitment to free market policies that had proved its most attractive feature during the post-war period.

An FDP switch to the SPD would be difficult to carry through politically, particularly as a SPD–FDP coalition would need the support of the Greens to gain a majority of Bundestag seats. Such a sharp change of allegiance by the FDP, although motivated by the desire to increase its chances of survival, might increase the danger of non-representation after the next elections in 1998.

● **Towards a Grand Coalition?**

Even though the new Kohl government will be less unstable than some commentators initially affirmed, it will be relatively weak. Room for radical legislative initiative will be tightly circumscribed. This affects above all the field of economic policy, where tough action is needed to cut government spending and restructure the over-generous social security system. The coalition's position is particularly undermined by the SPD's majority in the second chamber or federal council, the Bundesrat (representing the state or Land governments), which can block legislation affecting Länder interests, especially tax law. If the Kohl government meets mid-term difficulties between 1994 and 1998, a possible way of forming a broadly-based majority to push through unpopular economic action would be through the formation of a Grand Coalition with the SPD. In some ways, in view of the SPD's hold over the Bundesrat, the new Kohl government will already be behaving like a *de facto* Grand Coalition.

Both Kohl and Scharping indicated before the election that, although this was not their desired outcome, they would have been willing to serve in a Grand Coalition in the event of a 'hung' parliament. The SPD clearly favours the possibility of a Grand Coalition as a means of preparing itself for power after being in opposition since 1982. The only previous example of this genre of alliance, the 1966–69 Grand Coalition, was associated with a polarisation of politics which shifted opposition voters towards the far-right. The poor showing of the far-right republican party in the 1994 election, however, lowers anxieties on that score, and therefore makes a Grand Coalition more likely.

- **International policies**

Kohl declared after the October 1994 election that his commitment to press ahead with European integration would be unaffected by the polling result. However, for all Kohl's credentials as a supporter of European union, the slenderness of his margin will add to reasons for caution over further extension of supranational European decision-making. Kohl will need to tread a narrow dividing line between 'deepening' and 'widening' the EC during the coming legislative period. Additionally, the SPD's increased strength in the Bundestag and its majority in the Bundesrat will give the party more leverage to make felt its greater scepticism over the Maastricht treaty.

On the question of the foreign peace-keeping role of the Bundeswehr (armed forces) outside the Nato area, legal hurdles to 'out of area' deployment were overcome in a ruling by the constitutional court in July 1994. However, the government will make only cautious use of this new-found freedom to deploy the Bundeswehr abroad. The conflict in the former Yugoslavia has helped to make German public opinion still more sceptical about the West's ability to use force to bring peace to war-torn parts of the world. Since deployment for specific actions is subject to a majority vote in the Bundestag, the SPD's stance will be crucial. However, the SPD favours a highly restrictive policy on Bundeswehr deployment, ruling out any question of sending the army to take part in operations like the 1991 Gulf war. As in economic and European policy, the SPD's much stronger parliamentary position compared with 1990 will make it a force to be reckoned with.

Index